Beyond Free Markets

Beyond Free Markets

The Revival of
Activist Economics

Marc Levinson

Lexington Books

D.C. Heath and Company/Lexington, Massachusetts/Toronto

Library of Congress Cataloging-in-Publication Data

Levinson, Marc.
    Beyond free markets.

    Includes bibliographies and index.
    1. Economics.   2. Keynesian economics.   3. Industry
and state—United States.   4. United States—Economic
policy—1981–   . I. Title.
HB87.L45   1988   388.973   87-45775
ISBN 0-669-16971-4 (alk. paper)

Published simultaneously in Canada
Printed in the United States of America
International Standard Book Number: 0-669-16971-4
Library of Congress Catalog Card Number: 87-45775

The paper used in this publication meets the minimum requirements of
American National Standard for Information Science—Permanence
of Paper for Printed Library Materials, ANSI Z39.48-1984.

ISBN 0-669-16971-4

88   89   90   91   92   8   7   6   5   4   3   2   1

*For Aaron, whose cheerful presence
accompanied the writing of this book,
and for Rebecca, whose impending arrival
accelerated its completion.*

Contents

Acknowledgments

This exploration of new and relatively little-known ideas in economics had its origins in a series of articles published in *Dun's Business Month* and in its successor, *Business Month,* during 1986 and 1987. Preparing these articles, which examined the work of academic economists in far more detail than is normally possible in a widely circulated business magazine, provided me the opportunity to meet many of the researchers whose work is discussed in this book. Almost all of them willingly accepted the questions and objections of a nonspecialist invading their territory with a noteworthy patience, and I am grateful for their cooperation.

I would particularly like to acknowledge the support of Arlene Hershman and Gerald Rosen, who served as editor and executive editor, respectively, of *Business Month* and *Dun's Business Month* during my tenure there. Economists George A. Akerlof of the University of California at Berkeley, and N. Gregory Mankiw and Lawrence H. Summers of Harvard University read and offered extremely useful comments upon portions of the manuscript, although they of course bear no responsibility for its conclusions. Donna Zerwitz of the National Bureau of Economic Research has been helpful in keeping me aware of the work being undertaken by the many scholars associated with the Bureau. Most important of all was the help of my wife, Kay Levinson, without whose support and encouragement this book would have been abandoned long ago.

Introduction

E conomic activism is out of fashion. In almost all the advanced
industrial economies of the capitalist world, the belief that the
government bears responsibility for keeping interest rates low, employment high, output growing, and prices stable has given way to
a much more modest understanding of the public sector's role. With
the administrations of Ronald Reagan in the United States and
Margaret Thatcher in Great Britain taking the lead, country after
country has deliberately sought to diminish government participation in economic affairs, allowing market forces rather than public
officials to make crucial economic decisions. Deregulation, privatization, capital formation, lower tax rates, and smaller budgets are
the rallying cries.

This political trend, which defines government as the enemy of
economic growth and the private sector as the source of all prosperity, has rested on elaborate economic foundations. For over a
decade, economists committed to the proposition that the best government is a small and passive government have dominated economic science. Their research, based on a rigorous mathematical
understanding of the conditions for maximum economic efficiency
and economic welfare, has not only lent intellectual respectability
to what were once the views of an extreme antigovernment fringe,
but has also created new arguments in favor of government nonintervention. Against this rapidly growing body of research based on
a unified and comprehensive economic theory, the long-standing intellectual case for an activist government began to crumble. Political
parties whose basic thesis was that government could improve the
quality of people's lives, whether they were called Democrats or
Socialists, Labourites or Liberals or Social Democrats, came to be
seen as defenders of anachronistic, ineffective, scientifically unsound ideas.

Since the mid-1980s, however, a rigorous but less ideological sort of economic analysis has been making a quiet comeback. Building on the scientific methodology of the free market theorists but adopting a more complex and realistic set of economic assumptions, economists working in widely diverse fields are demonstrating that the case for leaving economic decisions to the free market is by no means clear-cut. They are showing that individuals and companies, each acting in its own best interest, may adopt strategies that collectively lead to lower economic efficiency unless the government intervenes. They are laying the groundwork for a new activist economics and for a revival of political faith in the ability of government to deal with economic problems.

While this new economic research points to the need for government intervention in economic affairs, it differs markedly from the interventionist economics of earlier decades. It offers strong reason to be wary of those who believe that simply unleashing private enterprise is the way to resolve economic problems, but it offers little support for traditional liberal political notions of the welfare state. Indeed, the new interventionist economists see a world that is messy and complex, one in which neither simple rules nor complicated arrays of government policies can assure us that there will not be another depression. In short, it challenges many of the preconceived ideas that have long dominated political life and suggests some new ideas that deserve serious consideration.

Why should anyone care what economic theorists have to say? The reason is simple enough: ideas matter. Although the tumultuous, politically charged arena of public policy is worlds away from the sedate classrooms and chalkboards of academia, every political debate is framed by the set of attitudes and ideas that we label "public opinion." But public opinion is in no way immutable. Rather, it is constantly changing, shaped by a host of factors: recent experience, advertising, the unpredictable presence or absence of charismatic leaders able to promote their own ideas. It is here that social science plays a vital role. By shaping our perspective on the world, theoreticians help us to come to new understandings of the way the world works. In the field of government, their constructs define the limits within which politicians may safely operate. Concepts developed in the realm of theory find their way into legislation and often have a fundamental role in shaping the actions of the nonelected officials who manage the government on a day-to-day basis.

This connection between theory and policy is rarely direct in a causal sense. Few laws are passed or policies adopted solely on the basis of some professor's idea. But in a deeper sense, social science theory precedes and legitimizes much of what a society allows its government to do. If, as this book argues, economic theorists are again coming to believe that an activist government is essential to creating the greatest possible economic welfare, their theories may well help build the ideology for a new generation of political and social leaders who are attempting to define a proper role for government in a democratic society.

The reader should be warned that the ideas put forth in this book are simply that. They are not, and are unlikely to become, conclusive answers to economic questions. Economic theories are intended to aid our general understanding of the way in which the world works, but applying them to specific questions of public policy is a tricky business. In natural science, the relationship between two events is often an immutable physical fact: when we see lightning, we know a thunderclap is soon to follow. Economics, however, does not deal with consistent phenomena in this way. There are too many changing physical, psychological, and statistical relationships involved. The fact that an increase in the rate of growth of the money supply has in the past often been quickly followed by faster economic growth, as theory would predict, does not mean that that same relationship will invariably hold true in the future.

Economic research proceeds through the complex language of economic models. A model is in essence nothing more than a mathematical statement of the way in which economic variables relate to one another. To the layman, such models are so much mathematical gibberish, with numbers, symbols, and both Roman and Greek letters strung together in incomprehensible ways. Often, however, a model can be "read" by deconstructing it, identifying what each variable stands for, and attempting to state in words the relationships that the model examines. The variables in most models are items about which governments or private researchers collect data, making it possible to "test" the model statistically. If the data tend to confirm it, the model may be accepted as a possible explanation of the phenomena it seeks to illuminate. This heavily abstract, mathematical, and ahistorical method has come in for frequent criticism from those who point out that models can never capture the complexities of economic life.[1] The criticism is true enough and is widely recognized as true within the economics profession. But the primary alternatives involve either raw empirical analysis or the mining of anecdotal historical evidence in search of common patterns. Neither approach offers a sound basis for making the sweeping statements about fundamental economic relationships to which economists aspire.

In the natural sciences (at least according to the textbook ideal of the scientific method), researchers are supposed to be able to check the accuracy of each other's work by repeating the same experiments in an attempt to replicate the original results. In economics, however, such replication is often difficult or impossible because an original data set cannot be accurately duplicated or because of subtle differences in statistical analysis methods from one computer program to another.[2] The accuracy of any researcher's work can rarely be confirmed or rejected definitively in a scientific way. Hence, economic theory develops in a wholly different pattern from theory in "harder" sciences. One researcher may seek to test for the same economic relationships as another but, using a different set of data, a different explanatory model, or a different statistical procedure, may come to a contrary conclusion.

Often, the major differences between two researchers' analyses lie in the fundamental assumptions that underlie their models. One famous and long-standing debate among theorists, for example, concerns whether individuals make economic plans only for their own lifetimes, or whether they also worry about the well-being of their descendents. The question of whether such a "bequest motive" exists is not one that can be answered empirically. There is probably no simple answer at all; some people worry a lot about the welfare of their heirs, some worry a little, and some are not in the least concerned. Yet it is impossible to understand fully how certain economic events—government budget deficits, for example—affect economic welfare without knowing whether citizens care that their children will have to pay higher taxes in the future to repay that deficit.

Economic theory, then, will not lead us to an absolute truth. But it can show conclusively that the "truths" propounded by many commentators on economic issues are not absolute either. Treatises putting forth the allegedly unchanging verities of economic life have proliferated in recent years, almost all of them in the form of paeans to the wondrous nature of capitalism. Invariably, their authors attempt to make the case that the government should keep its hands off the economy and let the private sector, through its unending drive to maximize profits, shape things in the most economically efficient way. A fount of highly sophisticated theoretical economic work has supported this contention. The lesson, driven home again and again as the purported teaching of economic science, is that the natural workings of unbridled free enterprise will create the greatest economic welfare for the greatest number of people and that government can only get in the way.

As the chapters that follow will show, that opinion is not the only scientifically sound view supported by economic theory. In fact, the conclusion that government intervention is always undesirable is a conclusion built into the research of most of the economists who oppose intervention. In building their models, they typically assume the presence of what economists call "perfect markets," a situation in which everyone is able to buy or sell as much of any product as he desires at the market price; in which all individuals in the economy have identical access to the information they need to decide on prices; and in which a full set of insurance and futures markets allows everyone to purchase precisely the protection he desires against risk and uncertainty. In this economically perfect world, they find no way in which the government can make the economy run better.

The economists whose work is discussed here start from a diametrically opposite position. They see the world as a place with imperfect markets, with oligopolies that attempt to fix prices and wages, with great disparities in individuals' access to information, and with woefully inadequate markets to insure against uncertainty and risk. Some of them even suggest that the underlying behavioral assumption of economics, that indivduals act to achieve the highest possible level of welfare for themselves—an assumption adopted largely for mathematical convenience—is untrue. In this imperfectly competitive, less-than-rational world, the economy will not run at top speed if left to its own devices. In various ways, the government may need to step in and help sort things out.

The first chapter offers a brief look at the development of economic theory over the past few decades in order to put more recent developments into historical perspective. Chapter 2 concerns the economic events that have occurred in the United States since 1980, events that have led economists once again to reconsider the truth of the maxim that the government that governs least governs best. The subsequent chapters then trace the findings of this new research in several different fields of economics and suggest some of their implications for the way government involved itself in economic affairs.

In many cases, the findings reported here may seem puzzling to readers accustomed to the timeworn political debates over economic policy. For example, when there are public demands that the government "do something" about unemployment, that "something" almost always involves spending money. But as chapter 4 points out, the often heated discussions about whether higher public spending is desirable may be irrelevant to the causes of long-term unemployment. It is the self-interested decisions of individual employers that lie behind much of the unemployment problem, economists now believe. To help alleviate the problem, the government must focus on helping disseminate information about workers' abilities and providing incentives for good worker performance, rather than on pumping up the overall level of spending.

A similarly complex set of problems arises with respect to the financial markets, which play an increasingly important role in almost all countries with market economies. These markets, as chapter 6 discusses, do not always work optimally; for a variety of reasons, they end up allocating economic resources in ways that will not result in the greatest possible output of economic wealth. But although the problem is easy to state, it is not so easy to pinpoint ways in which government involvement can improve the situation. Again, many of the issues involve the adequacy of information, a problem that is difficult for laws and regulations to address.

A concluding chapter attempts to extract the common themes from these diverse lines of economic research and to suggest their implications for the way we look at the world. This is an analysis that will be of little comfort to political activists of either liberal or conservative stripe, for it offers no simple answers to the policy issues they must deal with on a daily basis. Instead, it provides a reminder of the complex array of factors that must be considered in designing answers to the difficult demands facing government in the modern world, factors such as risk, incentives, inadequate information, and strategic behavior.

The economic work considered here in no way constitutes a "school," and it as yet supports no overarching theory of economic behavior. Many of its findings remain highly controversial and speculative, and may well be revised in the light of further research. Nor do its proponents have partisan political axes to grind. A surprising number of the economists whose work is mentioned in this book view themselves strictly as theoreticians who have little interest in whatever immediate policy implications their work may have. Most of them, having acquired the caution expected of a scientist, believe their work to be in a preliminary stage and remain reluctant to press their conclusions upon the public. Their ideas have only one thing in common: by focusing on an economically imperfect world, these economists offer a rich and radically new understanding of the way our economy works.

1
The Rise of the Free Marketeers

M uch to the frustration of noneconomists, economics rarely offers unambiguous answers to the concrete questions that preoccupy the public. It cannot foresee how quickly the gross national product will grow next year, or reveal ways to eliminate unemployment, or even specify whether the Federal Reserve Board should raise interest rates this week rather than next. But the way economists look at the questions that preoccupy people in their daily lives profoundly affects the way those questions are understood by politicians, journalists, business leaders, and voters. By altering the lens through which the public looks at the major issues the country faces, changes in abstract economic theories may well be precursors of changes in public attitudes that will eventually be felt on the political scene. Within the living memory of many Americans, the development in the 1930s of economic theories showing how an economy could fall into a long-lasting depression without government intervention contributed to broad public support for the growth of the welfare state over four decades. Conversely, new theories of the 1960s and 1970s destroyed the illusion that government fine tuning could smooth the economy's course, helping create the small-government climate that reinvigorated politically conservative parties in almost all industrial countries during the 1980s.

In the late 1980s yet another shift in economic theory, still widely unrecognized, seems destined to have political consequences of its own. Economic research is swinging away from the course it has followed for two decades, a course leading to the general conclusion that almost any problem can be best resolved by the workings of the market, without the government's intervention. As a reaction to the excesses of free markets, a new line of scientific investigation has emerged to support the much maligned view that an activist government is desirable, or even necessary, to help the economy run better. In the process, it is suggesting new types of government programs and policies—not a return to the free-spending days of Lyndon Johnson's Great Society in the United States or Harold Wilson's Labour government in Britain, but very different from the automatic inclination to keep hands off and let the private sector handle things, demonstrated by Ronald Reagan in the United States, Margaret Thatcher in Britain, Brian Mulroney in Canada, and Jacques Chirac in France. As Harvard University professor Benjamin M. Friedman has observed, "There's a new interventionist mood. The place you can chart that is in the research people are doing. The smart young guys are no longer trying to write dissertations saying government policies can have no effect. They're looking for explanations why . . . government policies can have an effect."[1]

The public's understanding of the lessons of economics, however, lags far behind the current state of research within the economics profession. In the popular and business press, in the classrooms where Economics 101 is taught, and in government circles around the world, the impression persists that minimal government intervention in the economy has been proved the way to maximize a nation's economic welfare. In the United States, Europe, and Latin America, a growing network of research institutions with admitted free market biases churns out paper after paper showing how free markets can resolve almost any economic problem better than the efforts of public officials, lending a scientific luster to the antigovernment crusade. "We need to get government off our backs, to clip the wings of the bureaucracy, to deregulate, to privatize, to cut federal spending, to decentralize political power, to reduce tax rates, to restore fiscal discipline," argued economist James M. Buchanan, a professor at one such free market–oriented institution, George Mason University, shortly after receiving the Nobel Prize in economics in 1986.[2] Citing the growing agreement among economists that individuals anticipate government actions in ways that may effectively counteract them, *Forbes* magazine even bid "good-bye to the illusion of active government management" of the economy.[3]

The intellectual supremacy of free-market ideas has been promoted by an outpouring of books and articles, many of them financed by foundations supportive of politically conservative causes, that advocate leaving almost all decisions in the economic realm to the private sector.[4] Many academic theorists have developed models that illustrate the same point. Even the careful student of the economic literature may be pardoned for believing that the intellectual battle is over and that believers in unrestrained capitalism are victorious. In the debate over the proper role for government, economist William Allen proclaimed in 1987, "Intellectually, analytically, the small government, private property, price-directed economy types have won."[5]

But that claim of intellectual victory is premature. Every revolution contains the seeds of a counterrevolution, and the antigovernment revolution in economics is no exception. The strong theoretical conclusion that government cannot make the economy function better remains undisputed when applied to the archetypal free market economy—an economy in which perfect competition prevails, in which everyone seeks only to maximize profits, in which all individuals have complete access to the information they need to decide on their offers to buy or sell, and in which a full set of insurance and futures markets allows everyone to purchase full protection against every type of risk and uncertainty. But in the messier world in which we live, that perfectly competitive economy is nowhere to be found. In the absence of perfect competition, the case for leaving all economic decisions solely to the choices made by ⌣ individual economic actors quickly collapses. In this imperfectly competitive, less than rational world, the economy will not run at top speed if left to its own devices. The private sector, to be sure, can do far better than the government at managing individual businesses and at making the hundreds of millions of decentralized decisions that occur in a modern economy each day. But it does not follow from that premise that those many individual choices always add up to the healthiest possible economy or to the fastest rate of economic growth. In various ways, the government may need to step in and help sort things out.

Government intervention in economic affairs, of course, is as old as the concept of government itself. By minting coinage, building roads, taxing imports, and waging war to protect trade routes, all governments fulfill economic functions. But the questions that now dominate the debate about government's proper role, such as whether government action can limit the extent of unemployment or keep interest rates low, were generally unimportant in rural societies in which most people lived outside the cash economy. It was the industrialization of Britain in the eighteenth century that made the issue vital. The barons of the newly established textile industry wanted freedom from government restraints, allowing any Englishman to enter the business without royal sanction, allowing factories to hire workers at whatever wage was necessary, and allowing mill owners to break up labor organizations that might conspire to bring about cooperation rather than competition among workers seeking jobs and thus drive wages up. To promote this view, they encouraged the work of such political economists as Adam Smith, who argued that laissez-faire government would allow individuals to create the maximum economic wealth.

Initially, mill owners were not eager for foreign competition, and they supported mercantilist philosophers who implored king and Parliament to increase the island's economic welfare by banning imports of cloth into Britain and its colonies and by barring the colonies from manufacturing cloth themselves. Once these measures had established Britain as the world's lowest-cost producer of wool and cotton cloth, however, the mercantilist philosophy posed a problem: if other countries followed the same approach, they too would build up powerful textile industries in competition with Britain's. Mercantilism was abandoned, and support for a minimum of government interference with any private economic decisions quickly became the dominant philosophy of the nascent science of economics in Britain and the United States.

This noninterventionist view, which Karl Marx soon termed the "classical economics," defined government's role as the establishment and maintenance of the basic rules within which private enterprise competed. Government was charged only with defending the country against foreign enemies; with making sure that no companies or workers interfered with competition by forming monopolies, cartels, or unions; with enforcing contracts; and with keeping prices stable, so that long-term business relationships could proceed without worry that inflation or deflation would disadvantage one of the partners. Within that framework, private entrepreneurs were encouraged to operate without restraint, increasing the economy's output by their own personal drives to acquire wealth. Anything the government might do to interfere with the system, such as regulating working conditions or seeking to alleviate poverty, would inhibit that wealth creation. If a nation came upon economic hard times, correcting the situation was believed not to lie within the government's power. The classical economists considered depressions an inevitability, a time of economic adjustment after which growth would surely resume.

This fatalistic understanding of economic life dominated economic thought up until the Great Depression. The only government policy required to maintain a healthy economy, in the classical view, was to back each coin or note with a quantity of gold set aside in a government vault—a policy that would inhibit the expansion of the money supply and, not coincidentally, make sure that the debts owed by the less prosperous members of society would not be wiped away by inflation. While it attracted sharp criticism from those unwilling to believe that government was helpless to alleviate poverty and hunger, classical economics maintained a powerful sway over government policymakers and business leaders. By the twentieth century, most economists understood that the case for such laissez-faire policies was not absolute. Some problems would clearly never be taken care of by markets alone. If vaccination against contagious disease were simply left to the marketplace, some individuals might decide that it was not worth the expense—a decision that might be individually sensible but socially costly, because others might be more likely to contract the disease as a result. Leaving national defense up to voluntary contributions by interested individuals would result in inadequate defense spending, because no one would have incentives to give without assurances that other citizens would not "free ride," enjoying the benefits of their contributions without sharing the costs. In such cases, the need for government involvement was conceded. But such obvious examples of market failure were relatively few. The major intellectual challenge to the classicists did not appear until the 1930s, when the work of the British economist John Maynard Keynes fundamentally changed the way the world looks at the role of government.

Keynes rejected the classical picture of a self-correcting economy in which wages and prices will fall and rise freely with each change in supply and demand, maintaining full employment of the economy's resources. Instead, he contended, an economy moves in a cycle from boom to bust. In good times, overoptimistic expectations lead investors to pump too much capital into new buildings and production machinery. This feverish activity drives up interest rates, but at the same time the surplus of investment means that individual investors earn less of a return than they had hoped. Eventually, the combination of high interest rates and low returns chokes off investment spending, throwing the economy into decline.

That story would satisfy a classical economist too. But where a classicist would argue that the investment bust will bring interest rates down so far that economic growth will be rekindled, Keynes demurred. If an economy were in such a deep depression that consumers had no money to spend, he believed, no interest rate would be low enough to induce a manufacturer into risking his money on new factories and machinery. Private investment would not increase to restimulate the economy, as free market theory argued. In that case, government must step in to help, running budget deficits if necessary in order to pump more money into the economy. Government purchases would directly induce some business investment to fill government orders, and would boost incomes and consumer spending sufficiently to encourage new investment in other sectors. "The duty of ordering the current volume of investment cannot safely be left in private hands," Keynes wrote.[6]

The Keynesian economic analysis included a major psychological element foreign to classical economics. Keynes decisively rejected the view that individuals always operate as rational economic actors, correctly calibrating the potential economic gains and losses from their actions. Instead, he argued that irrational behavior has much to do with economic performance. Workers, for example, are usually more concerned about how their wages stack up against the wages of others than about the purchasing power of those wages. Successful entrepreneurs, Keynes claimed, are driven in part by "animal spirits" that tell them when the time is ripe to start a new business or expand a plant. "[N]erves and hysteria and even the digestions and reactions to the weather of those upon whose spontaneous activity it largely depends" were said to have much to do with the level of investment, leading at times to excessive speculation. In general, Keynes asserted, "human decisions affecting the future, whether personal or political or economic, cannot depend on strict mathematical expectation, since the basis for making such calculations does not exist."[7]

Because of those incalculable psychological factors, Keynes believed an economy adapts to economic change far more slowly than did his more classical colleagues. Prices, he thought, move only haltingly, taking weeks or months to adjust to changes in supply and demand rather than instantly settling at a new level at which producers can sell everything they turn out. Wages follow the same erratic course: at certain times the economy may suffer from labor shortages if too few workers wish to take jobs at the prevailing wage, while during other periods high wages curb companies' demand for labor, causing unemployment. And even if the growth in demand for new consumer and industrial goods is slackening, a fall-off in investments to produce those goods may lag far behind.

These economic imperfections, Keynes suggested, create a constant need for government involvement in almost every area of a market economy, both domestically and internationally—setting interest rates and exchange rates, limiting speculation in securities markets, protecting key industries from excessive import competition, using budget and tax policy to stave off recessions. Although free, competitive markets work well enough at allocating economic resources that the government need not be directly involved in owning and operating the means of production, these markets fall far enough short of perfection that the classical dream of a self-correcting economy with no need for government involvement is a pipe dream. "[T]he characteristics of the special case assumed by the classical theory," Keynes wrote, "happen not to be those of the economic society in which we actually live, with the result that its teaching is misleading and disastrous if we attempt to apply it to the facts of experience."[8]

The Keynesian analysis was basic to the growth of the welfare state in all industrialized countries following World War II. As socialist, social democratic, or Christian socialist governments took charge in Western Europe and North America, the concept that a country's government was responsible for maintaining a stable rate of economic growth became a commonplace. Government programs to provide income to individuals, such as social security payments for the aged and extended unemployment benefits for those laid off from work, were designed to keep personal spending from falling sharply in the event the economy slowed; if these transfers from the government could keep consumers spending, economists hoped, business investment would not collapse and drag the economy into depression. Both government budgets and monetary policy began to be treated as countercyclical tools, to be increased when the economy appeared sluggish and to be cut back when excessively fast economic growth threatened inflation. In 1961 the noted Keynesian economists Walter Heller, Kermit Gordon, and James Tobin became influential economic advisers to President John F. Kennedy, and they persuaded the president that cutting taxes would put money in consumers' pockets and bring the economy out of the doldrums. Their formula worked, and Keynesian economics soon became the accepted wisdom in Washington.

This initial success soon led to excess. The Keynesian economists who dominated the making of economic policy in the United States in the 1960s had almost boundless faith in their government's ability to manage the course of economic events, a faith far greater than that of Keynes himself. The goal they set was to minimize the "performance gap" between the nation's actual output and the potential output which, they believed, could be achieved if government policy could help put all of the country's resources to work. In 1962 the president's Council of Economic Advisers proclaimed that the nation should be able to maintain an unemployment rate no greater than 4 percent without suffering inflation as a result. Although its creators later came to believe that that number was excessively optimistic,[9] the definition of 4 percent unemployment as "full employment" burned itself into the national consciousness, setting a standard by which the effectiveness of economic policy was judged. "Fine tuning"—the notion that the government could keep unemployment at that modest level and at the same time keep inflation in check by careful use of its spending, taxing, and money-creating powers—came into fashion, supported by the new science of econometric modeling. Computers, the hope was, could determine the relationships between past economic statistics and the ensuing economic events, and then use those relationships to predict the future precisely. If the most recent data on new job creation, business bankruptcies, and industrial production allowed the computers to foresee that the economy was likely to turn down in three months, the government would have time to increase its spending or boost the money supply and perhaps avert the slump. As Walter Heller claimed in 1966, "Although we have made no startling conceptual breakthroughs in recent years, we have, more effectively than ever before, harnessed the existing economics . . . to the purposes of prosperity, stability and growth."[10]

But the optimism that economists were smart enough to bring the business cycle under control proved unfounded. For one thing, accurate econometric forecasting proved to be an impossible dream; even vast systems of equations analyzed by highly sophisticated computers were of little avail in predicting economic developments accurately enough for policymakers to know precisely when and how to act. For another, the Keynesian theorists of the 1960s were concerned largely with maintaining and stimulating demand for goods and services, and neglected issues affecting the willingness of workers and investors to supply the labor and capital the economy needed to grow. By the 1970s, the stagnation of the supply side of the economy had become a major economic problem, one that traditional Keynesianism failed to address.

Third, while the Keynesians were economically correct in arguing that balancing the federal budget each year was neither possible nor desirable, their calculus did not take into account the political implications of opening the door to budget deficits. Deficit spending, previously known only in wartime and during the Great Depression of the 1930s, became the norm in the 1960s. The most ill-considered concept was what became known as the "full-employment balanced budget." Economists claiming to follow Keynesian teachings argued that the federal budget should be designed to be in balance with an unemployment rate of 4 percent. When unemployment is higher than that, they contended, lower income tax receipts and higher spending for social assistance would naturally throw the budget into the red, a situation that should cause no worry. The reasoning may have been correct—but the assumption that a 4 percent unemployment rate equaled full employment was disastrously wrong. Unemployment in the United States has not approached that level since the peak of the Vietnam War, so the "full-employment balanced budget" proved to be a justification for perpetual deficits. The budget surpluses Keynesian theory called for to restrain the economy at times of high inflation, on the other hand, seemed impossible to achieve.

By the 1970s, "Keynesian economics," growing ever more detached from its theoretical origins, had become synonymous with deficit spending and the use of the government's spending and taxing powers to redistribute income from some groups within the economy to others. In the public mind, Keynesianism and American-style political liberalism were one and the same. But the idea that the government could stabilize the economy by judicious use of its powers to create and spend money gained wide acceptance among all political parties. The opinion expressed in 1970 by Paul Samuelson, perhaps the most prominent Keynesian economist of the time, was widely shared throughout American society: "We have eaten of the Fruit of the Tree of Knowledge and, for better or worse, there is no returning to laissez faire capitalism."[11] Even President Richard Nixon, a man of conservative Republican antecedents, was proud to declare in 1971: "Now I am a Keynesian."[12]

Barely had Nixon spoken those words when the Keynesian consensus was rudely ripped apart. In 1970, with the Vietnam War winding down, the economy had slipped into recession. Unemployment rose to over 6 percent. But at the same time inflation, which had risen because of heavy defense spending, threatened to spiral out of control. This combination of economic stagnation and price inflation, which inevitably gained the moniker *stagflation*, presented a challenge for which Keynesian theory was unprepared. Keynesians had always presumed that government policies that raised the inflation rate would result in lower unemployment, and they could not understand why high inflation and growing joblessness were suddenly going hand in hand. Their traditional remedy for unemployment, an increase in government spending, didn't work: despite enormous federal budget deficits in 1971 and 1972, unemployment dropped only slightly before climbing to 8.5 percent in 1975, the highest rate since World War II. Inflation, propelled by a dramatic jump in oil prices in 1973, reached double digits in 1974. Starting in late 1971, the Federal Reserve Board began expanding the money supply at a rapid clip, in order, some alleged, to avoid a recession just prior to the 1972 presidential election, but that too failed to dry up the reservoir of the unemployed. The Keynesian ideas that had led to strong economic growth in the 1960s seemed irrelevant to the problems of the 1970s. As stagflation threatened to become endemic, skeptics increasingly wondered aloud whether fiscal and monetary policies were suited to dealing with unemployment at all.[13]

The leading voice in opposition was that of Milton Friedman, then a professor of economics at the University of Chicago. Friedman preached monetarism, a theory calling for the central bank to adhere to a slow, steady rate of money supply growth in order to maintain price stability. Historical research had convinced Friedman that individuals' demand for money changed slowly over time, at a predictable rate. The central bank of each nation, he argued, should plan the growth of the money supply accordingly. By adopting and publishing in advance a simple rule to regulate the amount of money the government would print, the central bank could assure price stability, putting fears of inflation to rest forever.

That restraint, Friedman contended, is the key to long-run economic growth. If individuals are confident of the value of their nation's currency and believe the return on their investments will not be devoured by inflation, they will be more willing to make long-term commitments to productive activity. An economy with a firm monetary growth rule may face ups and downs of output or unemployment, but government cannot usefully combat them. Although a quick increase in spending or in the money supply may make the economy grow faster momentarily, monetarists believe, stable monetary policy is the key to the greatest economic growth over an extended period of time.

Friedman admitted that a monetarist policy of the sort he espoused offers no short-term solution to a worker who happens to be without a job. Monetary policy, he said, cannot deal with unemployment. But, Friedman contended, fiscal stimulus of the Keynesian sort is ultimately futile as well: government attempts to rev up the economy can have only temporary effects. Keynes had argued that inflation would reduce unemployment by bringing down the real value of wages and thus encouraging employers to take on more workers; Friedman pointed out that those beneficial effects would last only until wages begin to rise as fast as prices, at which point unemployment will rebound—leaving the economy with its old unemployment problem and a new inflation problem as well. The only way truly to tame cyclical unemployment, Friedman argued, is to adhere firmly to a monetary growth rule, which will generally smooth out fluctuations in the economy's performance over the long term.[14]

Throughout the 1960s, Friedman, Karl Brunner, Allan Meltzer and other economists of monetarist bent provided the major intellectual opposition to Keynesian economic policies. As long as Keynesian policies seemed to bring prosperity in their wake, the monetarist arguments against government intervention were widely ignored, and monetarism itself was treated as an extremist view. In the late 1960s, however, it became part of the economic mainstream, and Friedman himself even took a turn as president of the American Economic Association. Classical theory began its intellectual comeback.

Its strongest and most controversial manifestation developed under the intellectual leadership of Robert E. Lucas, Jr., a former student of Friedman. In a series of papers dating back to 1969, Lucas pointed out a major flaw in the traditional Keynesian analysis. The economic demonstrations of how government intervention could improve economic performance, he showed, were rooted in a static model of the world, in which no one changes his plans until the government has acted. In a dynamic world, however, individual behavior is bound to be affected by the knowledge, or even the expectation, that the government will change its economic policies in the future. That, in turn, inevitably affects the way those policies work.

Put simply, people will act differently today if, say, they expect the government to increase the money supply by a certain amount to lower interest rates in order to stimulate the economy tomorrow.

Rationally anticipating the government's new policy and the inflation it will likely bring, individual consumers, investors, and workers will all strive to avoid falling behind when prices rise tomorrow. There might, for example, be a sell-off in the stock and bond markets, as investors fear that inflation will erode the value of their holdings, and an increase in labor costs, as workers insist on higher wages to compensate for the coming increase in prices. These actions could negate the monetary authorities' efforts. The result will be that while the central bank's anticipated moves cause changes in the nominal prices posted on store shelves and in the interest rates banks demand, they will not lead to changes in employment, output, or the after-inflation rate of interest. They can thus have no real effect on the economy. Although most monetarists would concede that stimulative monetary policy can increase the economy's total production of goods and services at least in the short run (although at the cost of reducing economic growth in the long run), a rational expectationist would conclude that individuals adjust their expectations so quickly that not even short-term improvements in economic welfare are possible.

The rational expectations approach does not insist that government is unable to change the economy's course. To the extent that policy moves are unanticipated, they can have major effects upon the path of economic growth. If the public can be temporarily fooled as to how the government intends to act, an action such as an increase in the money supply may indeed stimulate the economy. But if policymakers try to repeat the trick in a systematic way, people will catch on. This conclusion suggests that there can be no "automatic stabilizers" of the sort Keynesians envisioned as the heart of a macroeconomic policy designed to provide full employment. Automatic stabilizers will fool no one and will therefore have no effects.

The best government macroeconomic policies, in the rational expectations view, are those designed to minimize unsystematic fluctuations in taxation, government spending, and the rate of money supply growth, because those unpredictable changes lead individuals to have incorrect economic expectations, causing the economy to be more unstable than it would otherwise be.[15] To that extent, rational expectationists and monetarists agree. But rational expectationists are even gloomier than Milton Friedman about the government's ability to increase the economy's output. For them, fiscal and monetary policies do little more than determine how much the economy's growth over the short term varies around a long-term trend that not even the most stable monetary policy can alter. As Lucas observed in 1982, "I think this economy is going to grow at 3 percent a year, no matter what happens. Forever."[16]

Contrary to the Keynesian view of a world constantly needing government help to maintain economic stability, both monetarists and rational expectationists, firmly within the tradition of classical economics, argue that the economy is basically stable and self-adjusting. In such a world, they say, prices are the most efficient way of allocating economic resources, even if they are not always as flexible as they should be. An individual willing to pay $1.50 for a gallon of gasoline, according to classical price theory, necessarily attaches a higher value to the item than another person who will offer only $1.00; if the price mechanism is allowed to function—in other words, if the gasoline is sold to whoever will pay the most for it—the result will be the enhancement of the economy's overall welfare to the greatest possible extent. Rationing, price subsidies, and other government efforts to interfere with the price system will result in the gasoline's being distributed among consumers in an inefficient way and should therefore be opposed.

In many ways, the rational expectations model has proved an even stronger attack upon the traditional Keynesian perspective than has monetarism. Its underlying critique of Keynesian activist policies is indisputably correct: an economic theory that assumes individuals will not adjust their actions to the expected changes in economic policy is on weak ground. Unlike monetarism, rational expectations theory does not offer a hypothesis that can be empirically disproved. While events in recent years have demonstrated that the correlation between money supply growth and inflation is not as immutable as monetarists presumed, similar real-world events have not challenged the underlying assumptions of the rational expectationists. And rational expectations theory can easily be incorporated into economic models, allowing economists to pursue work in a wide variety of fields on the premise that expectations will affect the outcome. In modern economics, an economist who does not believe that expectations matter will be laughed out of court.

Rational expectations theory, however, remains controversial on two different grounds. The first is its presumption that individuals all have instantaneous access to full and perfect information and can thus adjust their expectations *correctly*. In reality, because information is not always diffused accurately or completely, many individuals may not fully adjust their expectations to likely changes in government policy or may do so only with a delay. If government actions will fool many people, at least to some degree, they have far greater power to move the economy than rational expectationists argue. Second is the assertion, troubling to many economists, that individuals do not always act "rationally" in a strict economic sense. Economists like the assumption of rationality because it is mathematically convenient to work with, not because of its realism. Rationality assumes that people are motivated by nothing but economic profits, but in fact, a host of psychological factors—concerns for fairness, cognitive biases, personal relationships—may lead people not to be concerned about achieving the absolute maximum profit at all times. If that is the case, government economic policies can have powerful effects, the rational expectations critique notwithstanding.[17]

Within the economics profession, rational expectations theory has had far more influence than the monetarist theory in which its origins lie. But it was monetarism that captured the public eye. Lucas, Thomas Sargent, and other leading rational expectationists have approached their subject from a purely theoretical point of view, disavowing any interest in shaping an agenda for public policy. They have rarely taken positions on political issues and have not become public figures outside of the economics profession. Their work has remained known largely within the confines of academia. When the resurgent political conservatism of the 1970s created starring roles for economists who could offer the public new rationales for allowing free markets to operate without government interference, the rational expectationists did not seek that stardom. A handful of monetarists did. A monetarist Shadow Open Market

Committee held well-attended press luncheons twice a year to offer a monetarist alternative to the money supply moves of the Federal Reserve System's policy-making Federal Open Market Committee. William Simon, an investor and former Treasury secretary with strong monetarist leanings, reached a large audience with two best-selling books on the economy. And Milton Friedman himself became a star of the new conservatism.

Friedman had laid important groundwork for the conservative movement in his 1962 book *Capitalism and Freedom,* in which he argued that political freedom is incompatible with government intervention and regulation.[18] Those ideas had found few adherents during the prosperous 1960s, when the conviction was widespread that activist government could solve the unemployment problem forever. But in the political climate of the 1970s, these long-standing arguments for a minimal governmental role in the economy appealed to a broad spectrum of political conservatives, from partisans of the "tax revolt," to business interests seeking relief from government regulation, to libertarians who opposed government interference in individual decisions of any sort, including those of an economic nature. The essential monetarist concept of a firm rule to regulate the activities of central bankers was intrinsically attractive to those who believed society needed firm rules for everything.

Friedman's Nobel Prize in economics lent its luster to the conservative cause. Through a regular column in *Newsweek* magazine, his opinions on a wide variety of economic issues came to attract great attention. In 1980, he even narrated a ten-part public television series called "Free to Choose," funded by the *Reader's Digest,* Getty Oil Company, and several foundations well known as supporters of conservative causes, in which he presented example after example of how government regulation and intervention harmed the economy. As a critic for the Wall Street bible, *Barron's,* observed, "Every program returns, one way or another, to his central theme: that a free market is better than a government bureaucracy at solving problems and providing goods."[19] Only professional economists among his viewers would know that Friedman's suggestions on political matters were often expressions of what he termed his "social philosophy" rather than conclusions resulting from rigorous economic research. In fact, monetarist theory itself has nothing to say about many major economic issues on the conservative political agenda, ranging from regulatory policy to antitrust law reform. No matter. By translating the case for government restraint into language the common citizen could understand, Friedman restored the credibility that free market economics had lost amidst the hopelessness of the Great Depression half a century earlier.

2
The Reagan Experiment

The rigidly noninterventionist conclusions of the academic free marketeers were uncomfortable for many of the politically attuned intellectuals involved in the conservative renaissance. In political terms, they saw, strict laissez-faire economics had nothing to offer: a voting public concerned about inflation, unemployment, poverty, and other real-world inconveniences was unlikely to look with favor upon the assurance that such problems would disappear as soon as the economy returned to equilibrium. And the message of mainstream economists that curbing inflation would be painful was not one that the populist neoconservatives wanted to hear. For them, the question was how to wrap political conservatism in an acceptable economic cloak.

The answer was "supply-side economics." The supply-siders, whose leading academic light was the brilliantly eccentric Columbia University economist Robert Mundell but whose best-known figures were journalists or economists of little academic distinction, shared many of the laissez-faire views of the monetarists and the rational expectationists. Like both these approaches supply-side economics built on the basic framework of neoclassical economics with its emphasis on markets. Unlike them, however, supply-side economists offered a message of hope based on a psychological theory that purported to describe human behavior accurately. This simple theory was, as economist Arthur Laffer explained, that "people change their behavior when their marginal incentives change."[1] With appropriate policies to stimulate greater individual initiative and risk taking, government could bring forth a fountain of economic prosperity. Proclaiming what Herbert Stein, an economist with ties to the traditional Republican business establishment, called "the economics of joy," supply-siders declared that there need be no trade-offs as competing interests fought over the economic pie. Instead, with proper policies, the pie could be expanded almost at will.

In the supply-side view, the most critical problem facing the country was the economy's limited ability to produce goods and services, not—as Keynesians saw it—lack of consumer demand, nor—as monetarists would have it—unpredictable growth of the money supply. Stimulating supply was thus the key to economic growth. And the most important way to stimulate supply was to alter tax rates to provide incentives for more labor, more investment, and more savings. Government actions that could interfere with these incentives and thus slow the rate of economic growth were undesirable.

The mechanics of the supply-side world were simple. High marginal personal income tax rates were alleged to encourage individuals to consume rather than to invest in productive ventures that would generate taxable income. This, it was said, had led to a lack of investment capital and thus to higher interest rates for businesses wanting to build new plant and equipment. If the high cost of money should deter business from investing, the industrial base would quickly become obsolescent, curbing improvement in labor productivity and therefore slowing economic growth in the years ahead. Capital formation—the development of a large pool of savings from which businesses can borrow—is thus a critical economic problem. Attempting to stimulate capital formation, however, requires rejecting the basic proposition of monetarists and rational expectationists that government intervention cannot increase the rate of economic growth. By encouraging more savings to increase the supply of capital and thereby reduce its cost, the supply-siders contended, the government *could* make the economy grow faster. Thus, they advocated lower personal income tax rates to boost savings and reductions in corporate income taxes to increase the rate of return on investment.

The size of the government budget per se was not important, in the supply-side view, because if people could be convinced to save more, the government's deficit could be funded without soaking up capital needed for private investment. The details of budget and tax legislation, however, were seen as extremely important in influencing individuals' decisions to work and create wealth. Budget and tax policy, then, should focus less on the total amount of spending and revenue than on reducing regulation of businesses, eliminating activities that could also be undertaken by the private sector, and paring income transfer payments that provide incentives for people not to work. All of these measures would lead to higher productivity growth and greater after-tax incomes for workers, diminishing the traditional inflationary pressures from production bottlenecks and from workers' wage demands. At the extreme, Laffer even asserted that disincentives to work were so great under U.S. tax law that a personal income tax cut would stimulate additional labor and thus actually increase government revenues—an assertion made with no empirical evidence about how much labor effort any given cut in tax rates would stimulate, and with no proof at all that income taxes were so high that this negative effect on government revenues actually occurred.[2]

Although they unanimously condemned Keynesianism, supply-siders were less certain about monetarism. The monetarists' views on the undesirability of government regulation and the social welfare programs they accepted totally. But because they had no underlying theory of how the economy works, supply-siders were divided on whether money matters. Some, such as polemicist George Gilder, claimed outright that it did not.[3] Others, including Mundell and Jude Wanniski, a former *Wall Street Journal* editorialist who became a leading supply-side publicist, argued that monetary policy should aim at maintaining a specific price for either gold or some basket of economically important commodities, such as metals and foodstuffs, as the only way of imposing discipline on the Federal Reserve.[4] The dominant "supply-side" view, and the one adopted in 1983 by the Reagan administration's economic advisers, was that money supply rules should be combined with discretion to keep the economy on an appropriate long-run growth path, while avoiding fine tuning.[5]

What all believers in supply-side economics had in common, however, was a strong distrust of traditional economic theory. Indeed, many supply-siders viewed their distance from conventional, mathematically based models of the world as a strength, not a weakness. To them, "supply side" was a visionary approach, based on observation of economic reality, with unmeasurable dynamic elements that both the methodology of conventional theory and the static assumptions of quantitative economic analysis too often left behind.[6] Theory would just have to catch up later. Stirring himself into a religious fervor, George Gilder urged that supply-side ideas be taken on faith, as a revelation that could only be confirmed after the fact: "New knowledge does not come without a leap of hypothesis, a projection by the intuitive sense. The logic of creativity is 'leap before you look.' You cannot fully see anything new from an old place. The old law of 'look before you leap' provides only for the continual elaborations and refinements of old ideas that comprise the bulk of scholarship."[7]

The vagaries of politics rarely allow economic ideas to be neatly tested in the real world. In that sense, Ronald Reagan's landslide victory over Jimmy Carter in the November 1980 presidential election was a boon for economic science. As the conservative takeover swept activist officials from bureaucratic posts throughout Washington, advocates of unrestrained free markets seized the chance to put their economic theories into practice. The "Reagan Revolution" meant to prove that hands-off government, along with low taxes to provide an incentive for labor and investment, works best at maintaining prosperity.

Although his disdain for economists was well known—he once joked that economists were the Soviet Union's secret weapon in its struggle with capitalism—Reagan, more than any president since Calvin Coolidge, entered office with a distinct economic philosophy of his own.[8] His firmest belief was in small government. "Government is not the solution to our problem; government is the problem," he proclaimed in his inaugural address in January 1981. Reagan flatly rejected the Keynesian ideas that had dominated Washington for fifty years, including the fundamental notion that the federal government could stabilize the economy's ups and downs. By seeking to control the pace of economic activity, he asserted, the government "has sacrificed long-term growth and price stability for ephemeral short-term goals."[9]

The Reagan administration's economic policies were based on two fundamental tenets.[10] The first was the libertarian assertion that a market economy is a necessary condition for political democracy. If government is involved in making economic decisions, according to the libertarian argument, it will necessarily impinge upon the ability of individuals to make choices in their own best interests, thus reducing the scope of individual freedom. The greater the government's economic authority, the stronger its powers of coercion. If an activist government represents a constant threat to personal liberty, any policy is desirable if it reduces the government's role in economic affairs. Reaganites therefore pushed for privatization of activities performed by the government and for a lessening of government regulation of private business decisions.

The second tenet of the new administration in Washington was Adam Smith's, that unrestrained markets deliver better economic performance than do markets guided by the government. Programs that distort prices, such as agricultural support payments and many types of taxes, lead to misallocation of resources. Welfare programs, worker safety laws, and regulations on business activity make the economy less efficient and discourage individuals from creating new economic wealth. Strictly for economic reasons, in this traditional laissez-faire view, the federal government should shrink, not grow, and should restrict, not broaden, its activities. As Murray Weidenbaum, chairman of Reagan's Council of Economic Advisers in 1981 and 1982, explained after leaving office, "This shift in national priorities is based on the general proposition that private citizens do not need government officials to make their decisions for them or to direct their daily lives. Most people—workers, managers, investors, buyers, and sellers—know what they want and how to obtain it. Over time, the aggregation of these individual actions generally results in the most appropriate distribution of our economic resources and the highest levels of well-being."[11] Thus, there was only a limited rationale for government intervention in the economy. And when some event like the creation of an industrial monopoly or pollution that would impose costs on others made intervention unavoidable, the principles of free market economics could still be used to develop the most efficient way of dealing with the problem.

On matters of macroeconomic policy, Reagan administration officials were clear that the government's main job was to eliminate inflation so private individuals would have a stable environment in which to make decisions. The path to achieving that end, however, caused a deep split within the administration. The monetarists occupying key economic posts pursued their traditional argument for tighter control of the money supply. By announcing and attaining specific targets for money growth, they contended, the Federal Reserve Board could show the world that it intended to stop inflation and could thus force down inflationary expectations quickly. Nonmonetary reasons for soaring prices, such as changes in exchange rates or excess demand for the economy's output, were viewed as irrelevant. On the other hand, influential supply-siders such as Office of Management and Budget Director David Stockman and assistant Treasury secretaries Norman Ture and Paul Craig Roberts understood inflation to be only partially a monetary phenomenon. Its major cause, they believed, was taxation, which reduced the supply of goods without a corresponding cut in the money supply; changes in the tax law to increase economic output, they argued, would therefore serve to reduce inflation. In an evident attempt to meld these two perspectives, the official Reagan administration program asserted that slow money growth was a necessary but not a sufficient condition for taming inflation; along with it, supply-side measures to increase the productive capacity of the economy would avoid the very Keynesian bottlenecks that had triggered inflation in the past. Although they disagreed on the proper government response to inflation, both monetarists and supply-siders concurred in the belief that it could not be cured by higher taxes or government spending cutbacks to damp excessive demand. The "wage-price spiral"—the long-standing Keynesian story in which strong demand pushes prices up and forces workers to seek wage increases to maintain their buying power, driving inflation ever higher—was relegated to the dustbin of history.

Despite their differences over the role of monetary policy, the monetarists and the supply-siders within the administration had much in common when it came to macroeconomic management. Their common denominator, drawn from the classical theory handed down since Adam Smith, was a rejection of the use of the government's spending, taxing, money-creating, and regulatory powers to stabilize the economy. Where every president since Franklin Roosevelt had seen a need for government intervention to help the economy work better, Reagan blamed inflation, slow economic growth, and stagnant productivity on an excessive governmental role. As his Council of Economic Advisers viewed the pre-Reagan past, "The increasing role of the Federal Government in the economy—whether that role was to aid the poor and aged, to protect consumers and the environment, or to stabilize the economy—contributed to our declining economic performance."[12]

Monetarist and supply-side adherents also shared a distinct unwillingness to admit to economic trade-offs. Where Keynesians had worried that reducing inflation would cause the unemployment rolls to swell, both monetarists and supply-siders agreed that there is no relationship between the two evils, except in the very short run. The Reagan administration looked at the issue through the glasses of rational expectations: so long as the public believed that inflation would be reduced quickly, the process of doing so would have only minimal effects on employment. With the administration's program of slower money supply growth and measures to improve the nation's productivity significantly taking hold, the rate of inflation was projected to slow from 11.1 percent in 1981 to 8.3 percent in 1982 and to 6.2 percent in 1983, even as the unemployment rate was to *decline* 0.6 percent each year.[13]

The centerpiece of the Reagan program was the Economic Recovery Tax Act of 1981. In line with the supply-side argument that lower income taxes would encourage individuals to work and invest, marginal tax rates were reduced by 23 percent over a three-year period, and the maximum tax rate on capital gains was cut from 70 to 50 percent. Individuals were allowed to contribute up to two thousand dollars in pretax income to tax-sheltered Individual Retirement Accounts, a step that was intended to increase the national savings rate. As an incentive for more investment by business, companies were allowed to depreciate plant and equipment expenditures much faster than under the previous tax law. In the short term, the new tax law was bound to cut the government's income, raising fears of large budget deficits in many quarters. Many monetarists hailed the Reagan tax plan for that very reason: shutting off revenues, they contended, was the only way to force Congress to curtail government spending. Meanwhile, administration officials blithely proclaimed that the incentive effects of the cut would stimulate $250 billion annually in additional private savings by 1984, enough to fund both the government's deficit and private sector investment needs without driving up interest rates and "crowding out" private borrowers. Warnings from monetarists such as Thomas Sargent and Neil Wallace about the dangers of combining a large budget deficit with the Federal Reserve's tight monetary policy were simply ignored.[14]

The administration held true to its belief in a world without trade-offs: just as inflation could be cut with minimal unemployment, taxes could be cut without boosting deficits or raising interest rates. How was this magic to occur? By encouraging increased investment by business and more work and risk taking by individuals, "these tax changes will contribute importantly to raising the levels of economic activity materially above those which would be attained under present law," the administration claimed.[15] In any case, the tax program was only part of an overall economic package that, Reagan promised, would generate a small federal budget surplus by 1984. Ironically, it was left up to Keynesian economists—the very same people who had long been attacked by Reagan and his cohorts for their advocacy of government deficits—to worry publicly about whether the massive red ink in the federal budget would force the government to borrow savings that could otherwise be used to far greater result by private investors.

The Reagan budget reform plan, unveiled together with the tax package a month after the president's inauguration, boosted defense spending while imposing "a set of clear, consistent, and economically sound policy criteria" that could be used to justify sharp reductions in many domestic spending programs.[16] Many of the proposals were, in fact, in line with proposals by the free market economists recruited by the Heritage Foundation to examine federal spending.[17] Job creation schemes, alternative energy programs, and community development grants were to be eschewed in favor of allowing "normal market forces" to achieve those same goals. Subsidies for urban mass transit, exports, postal service, and other activities were to be discontinued, since they "have served to distort the market economy and have thereby contributed as much to the problems they were intended to address as to their solutions." Income support programs such as Aid to Families with Dependent Children and unemployment compensation were to be revised to create incentives for beneficiaries to return to the labor force, in line with the supply-siders' view that such marginal incentives were of critical importance.

Finally, the Reagan plan called for a sweeping program of regulatory reform. Murray Weidenbaum, chairman of the Council of Economic Advisers, had first gained national prominence with a study estimating the total cost of government economic regulation at $100 billion per year. Now, he advocated subjecting proposed regulations to a rigorous analysis of costs and benefits, using a three-part test. First, regulation should only be undertaken if a market failure precluded a free market resolution of the problem. Second, state or local regulation was preferable to federal regulation wherever feasible. Third, not only must a specific regulation have net benefits for society, but it must be the approach that maximizes those benefits. Despite this elaborate framework for making regulation economically sound, however, the administration made no attempt to hide its intention to avoid regulation altogether whenever it could. "Even if used as well as possible, benefit-cost analysis is only the second best solution," the CEA asserted. "The best solution is to respect the judgment of the private market whenever it is available." In such areas as antitrust law or even safety regulation, the judgment of the market was thought to be the soundest judgment available.[18]

It took less than a full term of office for these implausible prescriptions to be exposed as a hoax. The 1981 tax cut led to a strong economic recovery starting in late 1982. But this recovery had little to do with the "supply-side" incentives for capital investment, and even less to do with the predicted increase in the willingness of individuals to work.[19] It was, rather, a recovery driven by the demand of millions of consumers—particularly higher income consumers, whose taxes fell the most—who found that less of their weekly pay was being withheld for federal income taxes. Although the supply-siders designed the 1981 tax law to favor business investment in plant and equipment, those expenditures grew only 12 percent from

1981 to 1984, while consumption expenditures were increasing by a whopping 41 percent. It was precisely the sort of recovery John Maynard Keynes himself would have foreseen.

Nor did the supply-side program increase the rate of personal savings in the economy. What the tax cuts did increase was the federal budget deficit, from $79 billion in 1981, the year before the tax cuts took effect, to $212 billion by the time the cuts became fully effective in fiscal year 1985. The government's need to borrow to fund the deficit kept interest rates high at a time when inflation was coming down: for top-grade corporate bonds, the difference between the interest rate paid on the bonds and the inflation rate of consumer prices grew from 5.27 percent in 1981 to 9.16 percent in 1984. These extraordinarily high interest rate spreads attracted a strong inflow of foreign money, and the more that foreigners sought to buy dollars to invest in the United States, the higher the dollar rose. In January 1981, 1 dollar would buy 1.82 Swiss francs, 2 German marks, and 202 Japanese yen. By the time exchange rates peaked in early 1985, it would buy 2.75 francs, 3.3 marks, and 260 yen.

This high dollar was devastating to American manufacturing, far outweighing the benefits that the Reagan tax bill brought to manufacturing firms. Although American consumers were on a spending spree, the overvalued dollar meant that an increasing share of the goods they were buying were manufactured abroad. In 1981, U.S. merchandise imports were only $28 billion greater than exports; by 1984, the gap was $113 billion and growing, and by 1987 it reached an incredible $153 billion. Even as the gross national product boomed in 1983 and 1984, industrial plants were using barely 80 percent of their capacity, a level normally associated with recessions rather than recoveries. The 60 percent rise in the dollar from 1980 to 1985 caused the loss of an estimated 1.8 million jobs in American factories. Manufacturing employment dropped from its peak of 21 million in 1979 to under 19 million in 1986. Even the removal of many of the obstacles to labor market adjustment criticized by the free marketeers, including weakened union bargaining power, wage reductions in many industries, and a fall in the inflation-adjusted value of the minimum wage, did nothing to put workers in heavy industry back on the job.[20]

Agriculture was also hit hard by the new economic order. High real interest rates forced thousands of heavily indebted farmers to abandon the business, accelerating the long-standing decline in the number of farms. For many, the path led to bankruptcy: the value of farmland fell by nearly one-fifth from 1981 to 1985, leaving many farmers with insufficient assets to secure their loans. The high dollar placed grain farmers at a competitive disadvantage in their export markets, while opening the door for agricultural imports to grow 15 percent from 1981 to 1984. Net farm income, adjusted for inflation, fell below Depression-era levels in 1983. Agriculture-dependent businesses suffered as well. In 1984, purchases of farm equipment were at the lowest level since 1972.

Ironically, it was the sector least favored by supply-side policies, the service sector, that prospered in the early 1980s. Service firms, which generally use far fewer physical assets than manufacturers, received much less direct benefit from the 1981 tax bill than did more capital-intensive companies. They were also disadvantaged by the administration's budget program, which emphasized purchases of defense equipment rather than the child care, medical care, and education many service companies provide. But they enjoyed some advantages in the early 1980s that had nothing to do with economic policy, including relative immunity from import competition and access to a large group of unskilled workers born in the baby boom years of the late 1950s. All told, service companies created 13 million new jobs between 1981 and 1988. The largest share of them were in such prosaic fields as restaurants, nursing, and child care, where the ostensibly procapital policies of the supply-side program were least important. Over half the jobs created were in businesses employing fewer than one hundred workers, leading supply-siders to herald a boom in entrepreneurship due to the new tax program. In fact, however, those dramatic indicators of the vitality of small business were caused largely by the rapid growth of service businesses (almost all of which are small), the deregulation of transportation, and the increase in subcontracting of work once done internally by large corporations. Relatively few of those new businesses earned sufficient income to make use of the supply-side tax breaks the law generously provided.[21]

Without an economic theory to explain the all-too-evident fact that the economic leap of faith they had called for led over a cliff, supply-side economists could do little but blame others for causing the unbalanced economy of the Reagan years. Congress debated the tax plan three months too long, they asserted, allowing the economy to fall into recession. The Federal Reserve Board was too tight with money, crimping economic growth. Deregulation plans had been delayed or watered down. Inflation had fallen faster than expected, depressing tax revenues and leading to higher budget deficits than projected. And, most of all, Congress had failed to cut the budget. But all the accusations could not obscure the sad and simple truth. There was no substance to the promises of supply-side economics. Its assertions about the magical effects of changes in the tax code had been accepted without careful analysis, and they turned out to be way off the mark. The supply-side program just didn't work.

If the Reagan years provided a conclusive test of supply-side theories, they also offered an opportunity to test the basic precepts of monetarism. Since late 1979, when the Federal Reserve announced that money supply growth rather than interest rates would be its principal target, the money supply numbers announced each Thursday afternoon attracted nationwide attention. An unexpected boost in M1, the basic measure of the amount of easily spendable funds in the money supply, was the sign for a sell-off in the bond markets, as investors were wary of any indication that inflation would return.

Although money was the focus of economic attention, monetarists rightly complained that a policy of steady money growth hadn't been given a chance. In fact, the rate of growth in M1 did vary considerably from month to month as the Fed forced up interest rates to drive the economy into recession in 1981, then loosened the reins, allowing M1 to grow at a 13.5 percent rate from July 1982 to July 1983 as the economy came roaring out of recession. From late 1979 to late 1983, M1 was within its target range only

41 weeks out of 206. Monetarists both within and outside government were sharply critical of this approach, demanding slow and steady growth in the monetary aggregates. "The sole function of monetary policy is to provide price stability," insisted Beryl Sprinkel, then under secretary of the Treasury for Monetary Affairs, in a speech critical of the Fed in late 1983. Only monetary discipline would create a noninflationary environment and change the rational expectations of investors that more inflation lay ahead. If the Fed didn't clamp down, fast money growth would be followed by inflation within three to six months, Treasury Secretary Donald T. Regan warned in early 1984.[22]

But the long-expected inflation never happened. Even as the money supply continued to grow erratically, inflation remained dormant thanks to falling commodity prices, low wage increases, and the fall in import prices stemming from the sharp rise of the dollar. Repeatedly, monetarist scholars warned of an imminent outbreak of inflation if the Fed persisted. But from July 1982 through January 1987, consumer prices never rose at an annual rate above 4 percent, despite money supply growth that was consistently in double digits. The basic, mechanistic relationship between the money supply and prices postulated by monetarist theory seemed no longer to exist.

Financial deregulation, the huge inflow of foreign capital, and changes in consumers' demand for money to make purchases had all combined to alter monetary relationships that had been presumed to be immutable. The velocity of money, for example, fell sharply. With consumers turning their funds over less quickly, a given stock of money implied far less economic activity than when velocity was high. Deregulation blurred the distinction between the "transactions" accounts included in the Fed's M1 statistics and other types of financial accounts; M1 no longer offered a useful picture of the amount of money readily available for spending when consumers could also write checks on NOW accounts at savings institutions and money market accounts at mutual funds. And as international factors loomed increasingly large in the U.S. economy, many economists came to believe that monetary policy in the 1980s affected the economy more through its impact on exchange rates than through its direct effect on prices and interest rates. This important but poorly understood international aspect of monetary policy made the time lag between the Federal Reserve's actions and the economy's response erratic and unpredictable.[23] Although many economists still adhered in principle to the concept of a firm monetary growth rule to govern the Federal Reserve, the practical difficulties of specifying what that rule should be had become so daunting that even orthodox monetarists were rethinking their positions. By 1985, the *Wall Street Journal*, long an advocate of tight money, was admitting that "in an interdependent international economy . . . the monetary aggregates have become increasingly dubious as domestic-policy instruments."[24] Barely six months later, Beryl Sprinkel, then chairman of the Council of Economic Advisers and the leading monetarist voice within the administration, conceded publicly that the monetarist ideology just wasn't enough to explain the course of economic events.

Inevitably, the experience of the Reagan years renewed interest in the much maligned Keynesian model. Supply-side economics had proved to be a short-lived fad, and the underpinnings of monetarist theory had been severely challenged. Unemployment proved to be far from self-correcting in the way both supply-siders and monetarists had contended; the unemployment rate fell from 10.8 percent in December 1982 to 7 percent in 1984 but then declined very slowly as millions remained out of work. Nor did rational expectations theory seem to hold in light of the dollar's climb far beyond levels indicated by economic fundamentals. If the theory were true, the fact that everyone rationally expected a sharply lower dollar in short order should itself have caused the dollar to fall. But in practice, it seemed, something in the financial markets wasn't working right.

The shape of the 1982 recession and the 1983 recovery too suggested that government intervention in the economy could indeed be a significant force. It was an activist Fed, bringing the economy to a screeching halt by tightening credit in 1982, that brought the inflation rate down far more quickly than anyone had anticipated. It was clearly not a passive government, waiting patiently for markets to clear and for wages and prices to adjust, that gave rise to a consumer spending boom of unprecedented proportions in 1983. Stubbornly high unemployment seemed to go hand in hand with a stable rate of inflation: by 1988, with civilian unemployment below 6 percent, some economists were calculating it could go as low as 4 percent without triggering inflation, suggesting that there is, as Keynesians had long suggested and monetarists long denied, at least some medium-term trade-off along the Phillips curve relating inflation and unemployment.[25]

Other events of the 1980s also proved a puzzlement. A wave of hostile corporate takeovers posed the question of why the stock market consistently values firms less than potential acquirers do. A trend toward dissolution of corporate conglomerates, many established only recently, raised doubts about the laissez-faire proposition that mergers are inherently efficiency inducing. The apparent success of Japan's government in promoting the growth of selected industries suggested that free trade might not always be the optimal approach.

In almost every area of economic policy, similar doubts arose. The case for a passive, noninterventionist government seemed far weaker than it had only five years before. Inevitably, economic theorists could observe that the real world did not respond as did the neat market-clearing, welfare-maximizing economy in their models. So, with considerable caution, the practitioners of economic theory began to reexamine the theoretical wisdom of the past decade. Using the elegant mathematics popularized by Robert Lucas and incorporating his assumption of rational expectations, they reexamined the role of government intervention. What they found was that the case for an activist government could be demonstrated as cleanly and rigorously as the case for laissez-faire.

3

Activist Economics Comes Back

"**B**reaking a new eggshell today," economist Benjamin M. Friedman has observed, "does not restore to integrity another eggshell broken yesterday."[1] That, in brief, is the problem of economics in the late 1980s. The simple free market nostrums proclaiming that the only good government is small government have failed the test of the real world. But their failure offers little support for political agendas demanding drastic increases in the scope of social welfare programs, protection against foreign competition, and tighter regulation of airlines, trucking, and other industries. The fact that the "conservative" prejudice favoring laissez-faire policies in the 1980s was wrong does not mean that the "liberal" enthusiasm for government intervention in every area of the economy during the 1960s and 1970s was right. A new approach to understanding economic issues and their implications for public policy, one differing sharply from both these traditional "conservative" and "liberal" positions, is in order.

Like all new ideas, however, a new understanding of economics must rest on the foundations of the past. The free market ideas of the "new classical economics," whether in its monetarist, rational expectationist, or supply-side manifestation, or in some more eclectic form, should not be discarded wholesale simply because the theories built upon those ideas have proved inadequate to explain the world we know. Although the grand, overarching neoclassical theories may have shortcomings, many of the elements from which each theory is constructed contain important insights that accurately describe the way people and economies behave. If it is to be convincing, any new attempt to define an appropriate governmental role in economic affairs must incorporate the lessons of previous economic research, and must also show why those lessons, misunderstood or misinterpreted, have led to incorrect conclusions in the past.

The rational expectationists, for example, are clearly right in arguing that expectations matter. This does not mean that people always guess correctly what the government will do, or that they act upon their guesses with only the maximization of their economic welfare in mind. Nonetheless, public officials plotting government monetary or fiscal policies must accept the premise that individuals will anticipate those moves and act accordingly, thereby altering the very set of facts on which those officials must base their decisions. The Keynesian model of the 1960s, which envisioned benevolent government officials making decisions for the public good in the face of a passive citizenry, cannot be resurrected as a model for the 1990s.

Neoclassicists of all stripes are correct in pointing to the efficiency of prices in allocating resources, an efficiency that economists of an interventionist bent have too often ignored in the past. Any theory that seeks to justify an activist government must assign prices a prominent role in balancing supply and demand—and, when government intervention is called for, must offer a clear understanding of why a push from the government will improve economic welfare beyond what the price system alone could achieve. If the markets for oranges, haircuts, and dinnerware function well, why does a national economy—which, after all, is merely the sum of all of these individual markets—not always work efficiently without government intervention? Traditional Keynesianism failed to offer a convincing explanation; it asserted broadly, for example, that unemployment exists because wages in free markets are usually above the level at which employers' demand for labor equals the supply of willing workers, but it did not provide a logically consistent story to clarify why this occurs or why government fiscal or monetary policies can solve the problem and provide work for everyone. Without a firm base in microeconomics, the study of individual markets within the economy, no comprehensive theory of how the economy works will be credible.[2]

These two concessions affirm the correctness of important ideas of neoclassical economics. But they do not inevitably lead to the conclusion that active government policy cannot result in higher economic output and a greater level of public welfare than a pure market economy. Although the adherents of rational expectations, monetarist, and other free market schools have pretended that their analysis conclusively makes the case for small government, the same analysis, it turns out, can serve as the cornerstone for far richer and more complex economic theories arriving at diametrically opposite conclusions. It is here that a diverse group of economists, rejecting both orthodox Keynesianism's readiness to overrule market behavior and the inclination of laissez-faire economists to let markets operate unrestrained, has begun to build the case for a new interventionist economics.

Intellectual opposition to neoclassical economic theory is not new, of course. Despite Keynesianism's fall from grace in the 1970s, many economists have advocated an activist government, and a variety of schools of economic thought—neo-Keynesians, post-Keynesians, socialists, and Marxists among them—have offered sharp critiques of the classical worldview. With few exceptions, however, these economists have simply turned their backs on the free marketeers and posited their own alternatives rather than attempting a systematic critique of the neoclassical model.[3] As a result their work has remained largely outside the intellectual mainstream and has done little to dislodge laissez-faire ideas from their place of prominence in national life. The importance of a new interventionist economics built on neoclassical foundations is that it attacks the ruling theory head-on, exposing its intellectual shortcomings for all to see.

As it happens, the modern free market theories of economic behavior share a common, and fatal, weakness that their proponents rarely discuss. They are built on a very special set of assumptions about the state of the world. Take away that set of assumptions and substitute another, and the case for leaving all economic decisions to the marketplace begins to crumble. Examining those assumptions one by one will show why.

Perfect competition. Monetarists, rational expectationists, and other free market theorists all begin their stories of how the world works by imagining a world of firms and individuals driven entirely by the unending competitive pressure to earn the greatest possible financial profit. If, for any reason, one activity offers a greater opportunity for profit than another, even momentarily, outsiders will enter the field and, by competing for a share of the pie, drive profits back down. This, of course, assumes that big firms do not produce more cheaply than little ones—or, in economists' language, that there are not large economies of scale. If it is more efficient for one firm to produce and sell millions of units of a product than for many smaller firms to operate, the competitive economy will break down as small firms combine into large ones, forming monopolies or oligopolies. New firms will find it unprofitable to enter in the face of an established firm's market dominance, because the established firm will always have a lower average cost of production than will a newcomer. But when that happens and a single firm or a handful of firms dominate a market, the forces that require efficient operation become weak. In a world of imperfect competition, companies' prices, production decisions, wages, and profits will all be very different from those in a world in which competition is intense.

Abandoning the assumption of perfect competition and instead looking at an imperfectly competitive world opens the door to an entirely new perspective on economic behavior. With it has come the introduction of an exciting but bewildering complication into economic thinking: game theory.

Game theory is a branch of mathematics, originally developed in the 1950s, that analyzes the possible outcomes of situations in which people behave strategically. Its original applications were military. Game theorists first made a name for their science through their cold and discomforting analysis of the sequence of moves and countermoves that could cause a minor disagreement among nations to escalate into nuclear war. In economics, if perfect competition rules the day, game theory is irrelevant because strategic behavior has no place: if Company A disrupts the business of its competitor, Company B, it will gain nothing, because even if Company B is driven out of business, other firms will immediately step into the breach and keep Company A from raising its prices. But under conditions of imperfect competition, game theoretic analysis can offer a deep understanding of what motivates people, firms, and governments. Many economists, schooled in the scientific method of determining correct answers to difficult questions, find game the-

ory infuriating because it offers no firm conclusions, only possibil-
ities. Nonetheless, understanding the economy as a "game" can
shed considerable light on the failures of the free market.

Take, for example, the troubling matter of "overcapacity." In
many industries that require costly, long-lived assets, from shipping
to steel to petrochemicals, the total supply capacity frequently
exceeds worldwide demand, causing prices to fall so low that producers lose money. According to the teachings of free market economics, this situation will resolve itself as the least efficient firms
depart the business. Capacity and output will fall until supply and
demand come into balance at a level that allows producers to operate with profit margins similar to those in other industries. But in
reality this adjustment occurs haltingly if at all. The reason is that
from the producers' point of view, reducing overcapacity is a strategic game. If a company leaves the business, it must write off assets
before the end of their useful lives and lose any prospect of future
profits. If, however, it remains in the business and its competitors
leave, the reduced competition may eventually enable it to reap
large profits from those assets. Each individual company will be
better off if someone else departs the business, but no company has
the incentive to close up shop first. The outcome may be that everyone attempts to survive, wastefully pouring resources into money-
losing operations while waiting for others to fail. This economically
inefficient deadlock can persist for years or decades before free market forces slowly bring about a resolution. Governments, singly or
in combination, may be able to speed up the process of adjustment
by compensating the losers or simply by mandating change. If government intervention resolves the game and reduces the flow of
money into industries that the economy no longer needs, the economy will grow faster as a result.[4]

The overcapacity problem is just one of many examples of how
market forces cannot automatically resolve economic problems in a
world of huge, oligopolistic firms and institutions. In this world,
there is a clear role for government intervention. Policies to foster
or discourage carefully selected industries may be worthwhile, and
an active trade policy that seeks to protect key industries could
prove desirable. Not all government interventions, of course, will
be for the better. The choice of a specific government policy may

itself become a game among business groups, labor organizations, political parties, and bureaucratic interests.[5] Nonetheless, the teaching of free market economists that government should always keep its hands off is incorrect.

Perfect information. For markets to function well, economic actors, be they companies, individuals, or government agencies, need information—information about current prices in the marketplace, about risks, about the likely behavior of others with whom they are doing business, about changes in the economy. Information need not be absolutely perfect for a market to function; if some fact relevant to a building's construction remains undiscovered, the law of supply and demand can still work well in the construction market when buyer and seller negotiate a price. But every participant in the market must be able to use the same information in order to base judgments about how much to bid or ask on a single set of facts. If information is distributed unevenly, or if it is expensive, markets begin to break down.

The availability of information is usually considered as a given by economists. It is one of the "standard assumptions" that lie beneath most theoretical work in economics, an assumption that often does not even rate mention. In reality, however, access to information can be a serious problem. The effects of informational shortcomings can be seen at any used car lot.

Why is it that a new car typically loses much of its resale value after only a few weeks of use? The reason is that information in the used car market is distributed unevenly. Potential buyers of used cars invariably have less information about the vehicles they are looking at than sellers have. If buyers are unable to be certain about the quality of a given car, they will assume that any car offered is of "average" quality and will be willing to pay no more than an "average" price for a vehicle of that type and age. Owners of the best-maintained cars, who know that their vehicles are above-average but who may not be able to demonstrate that fact to buyers' satisfaction, will find the "average" price too low and will withdraw their cars from the market. That, of course, drives down the average quality of the remaining cars, and the cycle repeats. Owners of better quality cars will find that the best course is to keep driving them, and only the lowest-quality cars will be put up for sale. The used car market will not function well, even though the supply of and demand for used cars are strong.[6]

The used car problem is a microeconomic one. A simple government regulation, such as the requirement that sellers sign a legal statement outlining the condition of their vehicles, may be sufficient to restore order in the market. But similar problems, stemming from a lack of information, can afflict the entire economy.

Consider a banker. Inevitably, a banker has less than perfect information about a loan applicant. Even with credit reports and a careful investigation, he or she is bound to know less about a borrower, and about the riskiness of the uses to which the borrower intends to put the bank's money, than does the customer himself. But there is one surefire way to find out which loan applications pose the greatest risk for the bank: raise interest rates. The borrowers willing to pay the highest interest rate for their funds are sure to be those with the riskiest projects, because they know there is a good chance that their projects will fail and they will end up paying no interest at all. Borrowers with projects entailing little risk, on the other hand, know that the probability of actually having to pay the interest demanded is high and are therefore likely to postpone their borrowing until rates are lower. In effect, the riskiest borrowers will identify themselves by their continued willingness to borrow money as interest rates rise.

Because of the special economic role of banks, this phenomenon has consequences for the entire economy. During a period of strong economic growth, interest rates normally rise as the demand for investment funds outstrips the supply. But if an individual banker charges a higher rate of interest for a loan, low-risk customers will stop borrowing and the proportion of high-risk customers among his borrowers is likely to increase. In addition, each borrower is likelier to use lower-quality methods of completing the project than he would if interest rates were lower because he will have to cut down on costs if the project is to produce the larger return needed to pay off the dearer loan. For the bank, higher interest rates may thus translate into a higher rate of default, poorer-quality collateral, and lower profits than it would have earned had it charged less interest. A smart banker may therefore try to avoid raising interest rates to bring the demand for the bank's money into line with the supply. As an alternative, if customers' demand to borrow its funds outstrips the amount of funds available, the bank might be wise to reserve arbitrarily the available funds for low-risk customers who are well known to it. Government efforts to fight inflation by driving up interest rates will work very differently under such circumstances than in a perfectly informed economy. As banks respond to a shortage of lendable funds by rationing credit to their favored customers rather than by hiking their own interest rates, the demand for credit will not dry up as it does when interest rates rise. With credit demand remaining strong, inflationary pressures might not subside as quickly as they would if banks' possession of perfect information made it sensible for them to raise rates for borrowers.[7]

Although the lack of perfect information may inhibit the functioning of the free market, it is not easy for the government to improve the situation. The government's own information is usually not superior to that of the private sector, so it cannot immediately set things right. In some cases, laws and regulations that make it easier for individuals and companies to obtain accurate information can help the economy function better. In other cases, the government may need to offer financial help to people or firms that end up being the unfortunate victims of the market's lack of information.

Complete markets for risk. Is an investment that returns 10 percent better than an investment paying only 8 percent? The answer, as so frequently in economics, is "it depends." It is impossible to analyze this choice of investments without understanding the personal preferences of the investor. Those preferences depend, in part, on the investor's attitude toward risk.

Almost every economic action entails risk—the risk that inflation will be higher (or lower) than expected, the risk that a natural disaster will destroy a lender's collateral, the risk that exchange rates will vary unexpectedly, the risk that supply and demand conditions will be different when a crop comes to market than they are when decisions on planting must be made. While undertakings with higher returns generally entail higher risks, the trade-off is not exact because risks are often difficult to estimate in advance.

For markets to function perfectly, there must be complete risk markets so that individuals can protect themselves against any sort of risk to whatever degree they desire. In practice, however, establishing complete markets is impossible, if only because operating a market involves significant costs. An individual in the United States who wishes to insure his life for five hundred dollars may have difficulty protecting his beneficiaries to the precise degree he desires, because the relatively high administrative expense of writing a new policy means that few insurers are interested in such business. A farmer wishing in April to sell a futures contract to obtain a guaranteed price for the delivery of his corn crop on August 17 will not be able to do so, because no commodity exchange offers trading in a separate contract for each day of the year; if he wants to sell corn futures, the farmer will be forced to agree to some date less to his liking, such as August 31, because only by limiting contracts to a relatively small number of expiration dates will the exchange be able to assure active trading in each contract.

In most cases, the lack of complete risk markets is a trivial problem. The farmer will likely be almost as satisfied with a guaranteed price for his crop on August 31 as he would have been with an August 17 contract, and the insurance customer may find that a policy for five thousand dollars will cost him no more than the five-hundred-dollar policy that was his first choice. But in other cases, the inability to insure perfectly against risks can have major economic effects.

Take the problem of finding jobs for the "hard-core unemployed." An employer is often hesitant to hire a person who has been out of work for months or years, because the very fact that no one else has hired that individual suggests there is something "wrong" with him or her. Although the potential employer may have no information about any specific shortcoming on the worker's part, he or she takes others' unwillingness to hire that worker as an indication that doing so would entail some unknown but possibly large risk. If there were some way to protect against that risk, such as requiring workers to buy insurance policies or to post bonds to cover the losses from poor job performance, employers might be more willing to hire unemployed people. That might lower the unemployment rate. It would certainly reduce public worry about economic changes that could cause unemployment, since the chance of any one person's remaining unemployed for a long period of time would be lower.

But there is no economically sensible way to make bonds or insurance policies a condition of employment. Private insurance companies won't get involved because they have the same difficulty as an employer in determining how large the risk of the worker's nonperformance is. Requiring workers themselves to post bonds is not feasible because the long-term unemployed are less likely than other workers to have the financial wherewithal to do so. If anyone were to offer a bond or an insurance policy in order to get a job, the employer would have strong incentives to claim that the worker's performance was inadequate in order to collect on the guarantee. Because the problem of protecting against the risk of a worker's poor performance cannot be resolved, an unrestrained labor market cannot be expected to provide jobs automatically for every worker, and the problem of the hard-core unemployed will not resolve itself.

Rationality. A fundamental assumption of modern theories of free market economics is that every individual acts according to strict precepts of economic "rationality" to achieve the greatest possible degree of economic welfare at every moment, to the exclusion of any other motivation. With this assumption in place, economists can take it for granted that whatever economic choices individuals make are choices that maximize their own welfare. Any interference with free markets inhibits individuals' ability to make those welfare-maximizing choices and, in most cases, will reduce the total welfare of society as a result.

There are two reasons for using the assumption of perfect rationality. The first is that it is the only assumption that allows economists to draw a single conclusion about how people behave; the contrary assumption, that people are not perfectly rational, allows for a wide variety of individual behaviors, with no one general type for economists to model. Second, perfectly rational behavior is mathematically convenient, because economists can then predict how people will act when given any specific choice by writing down an equation and using the basic tools of calculus to determine its maximum value. Less than rational behavior is much more difficult to deal with mathematically, a fact that has discouraged many economists from attempting to incorporate it into theoretical work.

The assumption of perfect rationality, on the other hand, seems to have distressingly little relevance to the world in which we live. Such psychological factors as benevolence, boredom, a sense of "fair play," a readiness to "follow the herd," and a search for pleasure are important in motivating behavior. They are evident everywhere, even if they are mathematically inconvenient for economists.[8] These psychological factors may lead free markets away from the direction of economic efficiency and even, as in the case of feverish speculation on a securities market, lead them to collapse. And their presence makes a great deal of difference in the way that government policies affect the economy.

Imagine a banking system without government regulation or government insurance. Every financial institution is free to offer a different rate of interest. The institutions paying the highest interest to depositors will presumably be those able to obtain the highest interest on the loans they make, which means they will be the institutions holding the riskiest loan portfolios. So long as the government requires each institution to make audited financial statements available to customers, each perfectly rational individual is free to choose the proper combination of interest rate and risk to maximize his welfare. A risk-loving person may opt for 9 percent interest on his deposits, knowing that his bank uses the money to make highly speculative loans with a high probability of default. A risk-averse individual, by contrast, may gladly accept an account paying only 5 percent interest, secure in the knowledge that his bank puts the money only in ultrasafe government bonds.

If individuals were, in fact, completely rational, this totally unregulated system would be the best possible banking system. But in a world in which rationality alone does not govern behavior, individuals systematically tend to underestimate the risks involved in obtaining a high interest rate, while bankers may surrender to the temptation to speculate with other people's money. The result may be bank failures and the loss of depositors' funds. That in itself is not tragic: each individual depositor knew that depositing money entailed risk. If, however, the collapse of some financial institutions were to engender a general belief that banks are unsafe places in which to deposit funds, that perception could cause major economic harm to others because of the banking system's important social role as a collector and distributor of investment funds. Irrationality could thus have highly adverse macroeconomic effects, causing lending to diminish, unless the government steps in to assure individuals of the banking system's safety by establishing itself as a lender and insurer of last resort.

In doing so, of course, it must be careful that its very assumption of that role does not lead individuals to act in a riskier fashion, confident that government will bail them out if the going gets rough. But without active government intervention, the irrational behavior of individual depositors and lenders will cause the financial system difficulty in meeting society's need for a source of investment capital. The free market alone will not provide a stable source of funding for large capital needs if nonrational behavior is the norm.

The law of one price. Free market theories of economics depend heavily upon price as the means of bringing the supply of a product in line with the demand. The price mechanism, neoclassical theorists argue, allocates resources far more efficiently than any other method. Implicit in this argument, but almost never stated, is the assumption that there is a single "correct" price for each good at which supply and demand will be in precise balance.

In reality, however, the price that a farmer receives for his potatoes and the amount an oil dealer must pay for the fuel he distributes are highly dependent upon the way in which the markets for those products are organized. Under different sets of rules, the same group of buyers and sellers could arrive at a wide variety of different prices.

Economists typically assume that buyers and sellers deal in a huge market in which the price does not depend on the actions of any individual. Each buyer decides how many units he is willing to buy at each possible selling price, a number that, in most circumstances, declines as the price goes up. Each seller determines how many he will sell, a number likely to be small when prices are low and to mount as prices rise. Eventually, after repeated haggling among the thousands of buyers and sellers, the price will settle at some level at which the market "clears," with sell orders exactly matching buy orders. Every buyer purchases all he desires to buy at the single agreed-upon price, while every seller is able to sell all he wishes to put on the market at that price level.

But if the market doesn't operate according to those simple rules, buyers and sellers may well settle on prices different from the ones they would reach after such intensive bargaining. When sellers are required to post their prices in writing for everyone to see, economists have found, prices tend to be higher than in a market without posted prices because the give-and-take that is supposed to force prices down does not occur; each individual seller no longer has the incentive to lower his prices to cut a deal, because he can be confident that no other seller is doing so. Prices at a sealed-bid auction tend to be systematically different from prices at an auction with open bidding, at least until the participants in the sealed-bid auction have repeated the process enough that they can predict each other's behavior. And if the market does not have a means of reliably disseminating price information, it is entirely possible that the price agreed upon for one transaction will be quite different from that reached in another.

Without a single "correct" price at which each market will clear, there can be no assurance that the price system alone will lead to the most efficient allocation of economic resources. Consumers will buy different combinations of goods and services than they would at that ideal market-clearing price, simply because the prices they actually face give incorrect signals about the relative value of each item. Producers may turn out more of one product and less of another than they would with a single market-clearing price, misallocating their labor, equipment, and raw materials in the process. The laissez-faire economy, whose functioning is critically dependent upon the market-clearing role of prices, may be seriously out of order.

Each of these assumptions is taken as a given by economists who find no role for government interference with the functioning of the free market. If the assumptions are granted, then the neoclassical case for a noninterventionist government is difficult to crack. Its theoretical consistency, given these conditions, is impressive. But as economists have recently begun to discover, relaxing these vital conditions can lead to radically different conclusions about the state of the economy and about government's role within it. Under those circumstances, following the new classical economics will lead to results that monetarists and rational expectationists never anticipated, results that do not maximize a nation's economic welfare.

It is here that a diverse group of younger economists, schooled in the rigorous mathematical logic of neoclassical economics but skeptical of its assumptions of market perfection, has begun development of a theoretically sound alternative to the model of the free marketeers. By relaxing the rigorous but unrealistic conditions surrounding the free market model, they can demonstrate ways in which, at least in theory, an active government role in the economy can make the country better off.

Although their work is generally in the Keynesian tradition, by and large these academics are too young to have been involved in economic policy matters when Keynesianism was last in fashion. The intellectual godfathers of the movement, economists such as Joseph Stiglitz of Princeton University and George Akerlof of the University of California at Berkeley, have been practicing their trade for two decades but as pure theoreticians rather than as government policy advisers. Many of their younger colleagues now involved in developing a new approach to economic issues have earned their doctorates only in the 1980s. Their views are therefore distinctly different from those of the mainstream Keynesians whose ideas have been at the core of American political liberalism. These economic scholars have been heavily influenced by the events of the 1980s. Their own experiences over the past decade make them at once aware of the need for an activist government and skeptical of that government's ability to shape the world according to some carefully laid plan. They are interventionists but cautious interventionists.

In fact, they have little in common but a skepticism about the efficiency of the unrestrained free market. Modern economics is a highly specialized discipline, in which economists working on trade policy may well be unaware of common ideas linking their work with that of others in labor economics or monetary policy. There is no organized scheme encouraging economists to find excuses for big government, no single institution that has taken the lead in developing activist approaches to problems of economic policy. The longtime mother church of "liberal" economic policy ideas in the United States, the Brookings Institution in Washington, D.C., which is famed for its large-scale empirical studies, has relatively little to do with these new developments in economic theory. The economists involved are dispersed throughout the country, although organizations such as the National Bureau of Economic Research in Cambridge, Massachusetts, long known primarily as the arbiter of the United States' business cycles, and the Institute for International Economics in Washington, D.C., founded in 1981 to promote research on international economic issues, have provided opportunities for them to exchange and disseminate their views.

This general backlash against neoclassical theory does not even have a broadly applicable name. Nor is there a guiding set of principles, save a lack of faith in economic models that depend on perfect market clearing. The common characteristic of these new interventionist economists is a desire to comprehend the workings of the world they observe on a daily basis, with all its foibles and imperfections, rather than forcing events into a rigid theoretical framework based on some definition of an ideal world that has never existed. They reject the approach of those who begin with a mathematical statement of the most efficient economy possible and then insist that the world conforms to that equation. Instead, they take the neoclassical model and ask, "But what if. . . ." What happens to the well-known case for free international trade if companies are large and monopolistic rather than small and perfectly competitive? What are the economic consequences of securities trading if the stock market does not operate with perfect efficiency? What changes are there in the labor market if employers lack perfect information about workers? The answers they obtain, of course, are quite different from those that neoclassical economists offer as the economic truth.

Disputing the sweeping claims of the free market model turns out to be relatively easy. Having made a strong theoretical case that laissez-faire government policies are not always the best course, activist economists must face the far more difficult tasks of defining the specific ways in which government intervention may lead to a higher level of economic welfare, and of distinguishing those situations from the cases in which government should refrain from inserting itself into the workings of the economy.

4

Understanding Unemployment

W hy is there unemployment? Over the past half-century, no question has preoccupied economists more than this.

In theory, unemployment should be nothing more than a transitory phenomenon. Just as the prices of cars and haircuts rise and fall until supply equals demand, wages should adjust until joblessness is eliminated. But in practice, save for rare periods of labor shortage, unemployment seems to be a permanent feature of a modern economy. Reconciling the theory with this all-too-apparent reality has proved among the most difficult tasks facing the economics profession. As Canadian economist James W. Dean noted at the beginning of this decade, "The major theoretical challenge of the 1980's is to explain why markets in the aggregate don't guarantee employment for all who want it despite the fact that full employment in this sense is desired by all individual market participants."[1]

Although economists treat this question as a matter of theory, their attempts to resolve it are obviously important in the real world. Keeping people at work is a political imperative for every government, and a government's success or failure in reducing the unemployment rate is inevitably a major issue at election time. Exactly what steps a government can take to maintain a high level of employment, however, is a subject of constant dispute in the political arena. In developing policies to deal with the problem, political leaders must first come to an understanding of its underlying nature and causes, an understanding that is likely to be heavily colored by the lessons of economic theory. It is here that recent economic research has made a dramatic break with the past. Alongside the traditional debates about whether monetary policy, fiscal policy, both, or neither can be effective in stimulating the economy and increasing employment, a dramatically new literature has arisen suggesting that economists have been asking the wrong questions about why unemployment exists—and getting the wrong answers in response.

Traditionally, economists' discussion of unemployment has been plagued by a vexing problem: labor markets do not seem to work like the markets for goods or services. Markets for coffee or razor blades are flexible. If suppliers want to sell more at the going price than customers want to buy, the price will fall until supply equals demand and everything in the market is bought up, or, in technical parlance, the market clears. In theory, workers' wages should perform precisely the same market-clearing function as other prices in the economy, adjusting upwards in times of labor shortage and falling when there is unemployment, until everyone who wants to work has a job. If wages drop, employers will hire more workers, increasing the demand for labor. If wages rise, more people will choose to enter the work force, increasing the supply of labor. Eventually, wages should stabilize at the level where the number of people employers want to hire is equal to the number willing to work, leaving the unemployment rate at zero. There will always be a small amount of "frictional" unemployment, of course, as people change jobs. But if the labor market functions well, involuntary joblessness should not be part of the economic landscape.

Clearly, the labor market does not work as smoothly as this idealized version would have it, but economists have had difficulty explaining why. Free market theorists have tended to blame workers themselves. Robert Lucas, for example, has pointed to workers' unrealistic wage expectations, which are caused by poor information about what current wage rates are. "Why don't unemployed people get jobs as cab drivers?" he asks rhetorically. "I guess they don't want to. They have better things to do with their time."[2] Milton Friedman's bleak explanation is that in every economy, unemployment tends to some "natural rate" at which there is neither pressure to raise real wages nor to lower them. The only way a government can permanently curb joblessness is to reduce the "natural rate" by removing rigidities in the labor market, such as wage-and-hour laws, unions, or low worker mobility, that cause it to be higher than it otherwise might be.[3] The labor policy recommendations that stem from both Lucas's rational expectations analysis and

Friedman's monetarist views—repealing minimum wage laws, curtailing union bargaining power, eliminating the wage standards that must be adhered to on government-funded construction projects—have gained a prominent place on the conservative political agendas in the United States, Canada, and Europe, promoted with the argument that such measures will help put the unemployed back to work.

Most economists who are skeptical about the ability of "the market" to keep everybody unemployed trace their ideas back to John Maynard Keynes. In his *General Theory of Employment, Interest, and Money,* published in 1936, Keynes pointed out that wages are usually "sticky" and slow to adjust to changes in demand and supply. This rigidity means that the wages of people who presently hold jobs are usually higher than the wage that would persuade employers to hire everyone who is looking for work. Wage stickiness, which Keynes ascribes to both institutional and psychological factors, makes unemployment inevitable.[4] Traditionally, many Keynesians have supported inflationary policies to increase employment, based on the stickiness argument: although the face amount of paychecks will fall only with great difficulty, general price inflation will reduce the real, inflation-adjusted value of that nominal wage, causing employers to hire more workers. After the British economist A.W. Phillips offered his famous Phillips curve in 1958, suggesting that low inflation in Britain historically went hand in hand with high unemployment, the belief that there is a trade-off between inflation and unemployment became a prominent part of liberal political thought in the United States and of social democratic thought in Europe.[5] Many policymakers drew the conclusion that governments could eliminate unemployment altogether if they want to, provided they are willing to pay the price in terms of a high rate of inflation.

Empirical evidence has rendered both Keynesian and free market theories unconvincing as explanations of long-term structural unemployment. Lucas's assertion that involuntary unemployment is not a fact but a "theoretical construct" has become progressively harder to maintain through the 1980s,[6] as unemployment has persisted at double-digit levels in much of Western Europe and averaged over 7 percent in the United States. In fact, one result of rational expectations could actually be greater long-term unemployment, since if employers expect there to be greater unemployment in the future, they may be acting rationally by laying off workers now in preparation for an economic slowdown.[7] Friedman's contention that removing labor market rigidities would reduce the natural rate of unemployment, while partially true, has not worked out as predicted: although the legal minimum wage in the United States has steadily declined in value after adjustments for inflation, unemployment remains high among the young and unskilled workers who are most likely to earn the minimum. Meanwhile, in industries where unionized workers agreed to lower pay, such as steel and meatpacking, the labor force has continued to shrink, the opposite of what would be expected if wages alone determined employment levels.

On the other side, the presumption of political liberals that the government can always curb unemployment by expanding the economy and causing inflation was laid to rest in the 1970s, when high inflation rates in the United States were accompanied by unusually high levels of joblessness. The experience of "stagflation" showed that the purported trade-off between inflation and unemployment is a myth, at least in the long term. As Lucas and Leonard A. Rapping pointed out in 1969, the critical issue is not the *rate* of inflation but rather the *unexpected change in the inflation rate*. To keep unemployment permanently low, the government must keep inflation accelerating faster than anyone expects—an unappealing prospect for even the most employment-conscious politician.[8]

The strict rational expectations, monetarist, and Keynesian models of the labor market, then, have all failed the test of explaining actual economic events. They don't shed light upon Henry Ford's famous decision of 1914 to pay workers an unheard-of five dollars for working an eight-hour day, or upon Delta Airlines' practice of paying nonunion workers far more than their unionized counterparts at other airlines receive.

In addition, all three fall short on strictly theoretical grounds. It is hard to believe that unemployed workers remain ignorant of actual market wage levels over long periods of time, as the theory of rational expectations insists. The Keynesian claim that wages are sticky offers no convincing explanation of why wage rigidities persist. All three theories fail to explain why unemployment does not spread evenly through the labor force but is concentrated among certain groups of workers—or why one worker may be unemployed while another with identical characteristics is holding a job. Nor do they explain why employers typically deal with a lack of demand for their products by reducing the number of employees on their rosters, rather than by keeping employment the same but cutting back on hours.

Traditional attempts to answer these questions have pointed to such things as paternalistic employer attitudes, labor laws, or unstated but mutually accepted contracts between workers and bosses, all of which could keep wages from adjusting quickly. But economists trained to assume that individuals maximize their own economic welfare are instinctively uncomfortable with such ad hoc explanations of individuals' behavior. Why, after all, should an employer who bargains hard for the lowest price for real estate and raw materials not also try to pay the lowest possible price when hiring labor?

Thus, unemployment, one of the most basic economic problems in the world, has largely defied sound theoretical analysis. The explanations offered by traditional theorists of all schools have led to government policies that have failed to bring the unemployment rate down. But starting in the mid-1980s, economists trained in Keynesian theory but not wedded to thinking along traditional Keynesian lines have begun looking at the problem of unemployment afresh. Like economists from almost all schools of thought, they start from the proposition that the failure of wages to fall to market-clearing levels keeps some people involuntarily out of work. But rather than assuming that some noneconomic motivation systematically causes employers and employees to agree on the wrong amount of pay, they conclude that the cause lies within the employment relationship itself.

Employers, they assert, find it individually profitable to pay their workers more than the minimum wage required to obtain labor. By definition, however, this means that wages are above market-clearing levels. Each employer, of course, will hire fewer workers than he or she would at lower rates of pay. These higher wages will make each individual firm operate more efficiently—in

fact, economists call them "efficiency wages"—but they create a collective problem for society by leaving some workers permanently
out in the cold.[9] The reasons lie in the failure of markets that economists have only recently begun to examine closely, the markets for
information and insurance.

Suppose for a moment that the labor market operates perfectly.
All workers receive exactly the wage at which the number of people
desiring to work equals the number that employers want to hire—
the market-clearing wage—and wages adjust instantly with every
change in supply and demand so no one is unemployed. What happens to a worker who misbehaves on the job? The employer may
fire him, but in this perfect economy he will immediately be hired
by someone else at the same market-clearing wage. Since there is no
possibility that his indolence or incompetence will lead to long-term
unemployment, the worker has little incentive to do his job well.
The firm may end up with workers who shirk on the job, low output per worker, and a substantial cost to hire managers and supervisors who produce nothing themselves but spend their time making
sure that workers don't shirk.

In the face of this potential discipline problem, the smart employer will pay *more* than the market-clearing wage. With higher
wages, workers have much to lose individually by shirking because
the other available jobs may pay less than what they presently earn.
In addition, they face a serious risk of finding no job at all: every
employer paying more than the market-clearing wage will necessarily be hiring fewer workers than he or she would at a lower wage,
leaving some people who are willing to work at the market-clearing
wage unemployed. The possibility of being out of work for a long
period of time functions as an incentive for workers to do their jobs
well and not to shirk.

For each employer individually, paying this above-market wage
makes sense. A small increment in pay above the market-clearing
wage will lead to gains from increased efficiency and a diminished
need for supervision that far outweigh the higher wage bill.

To be sure, there are other methods companies can use to maintain discipline in the work force without paying excessively high
wages. Workers could be required to post performance bonds before being hired, so that shirking on the job would have direct fi-

nancial repercussions for them. Or employers could attempt to fine workers who misbehave. But from the employer's point of view, paying the higher wage is generally more efficient in preventing shirking, because it seeks to induce voluntary cooperation from workers rather than imposing tight supervision at considerable expense in both manpower and lower worker morale. From the workers' viewpoint, efficiency wages are also preferable to bonds or fines because they eliminate the risk that the employer will make false claims of shirking in order to collect the money.

Collectively, however, these high wages have spillover effects that individual employers need not take into account. By offering wages above the market-clearing level, each employer forces competitors to follow suit in order to obtain the best workers. With many firms paying high wages and therefore employing fewer workers than they otherwise would, the entire economy will consistently provide jobs for fewer workers. Potentially productive labor will remain unused, so total economic output will remain well below the level it could potentially achieve.[10]

In a perfectly efficient world, an employer would be able to adjust each worker's wage to reflect that worker's contribution to the company's total output. Often, however, it is difficult, if not impossible, for the employer to have perfect information about the job performance of each individual without spending a large amount of money to monitor workers. Workers themselves, on the other hand, are quite likely to be aware of their own abilities. If an employer reduces wages because of a drop in the overall demand for labor, the best workers, knowing that they are worth more than the new rate of pay, will quit first, because they will be aware of their superior value to other employers. The work force they leave behind will become increasingly inefficient as its best members leave, possibly driving the employer's cost for each unit of output even higher than it was before wages were cut.

This type of problem, known as adverse selection, is a frequent one in business when one party has imperfect information. If a bank raises its interest rates on loans, the best customers will be the first to seek money elsewhere, raising the overall level of risk in the loan portfolio and forcing the bank to raise interest rates still further. If an insurance company raises premiums, the least risky customers will begin to find it sensible to refuse the insurance, leaving an even higher risk pool of insureds, necessitating yet higher rates. Although he or she may not be able to tell which of the workers are above average, the employer can be sure that better ones will identify themselves by leaving if wages fall. Paying more than the market-clearing wage allows an employer to avoid this adverse selection problem and ensure the presence of above-average workers in his or her labor force. The decision to pay higher wages can thus be efficient for the employer. But because wages are so high, the firm will engage fewer workers than at lower rates of pay. If many firms do the same, the economy will provide too few jobs for the number of people seeking work. Again, the economy suffers from a problem of collective action: although each individual employer does what is best for him, the result is an underuse of the available economic resources. Unemployment is built into the system.[11]

Even if they are somehow able to monitor workers well enough to avoid the adverse selection problem, employers face significant costs of labor turnover. Workers earning only the market-clearing wage will be indifferent between keeping one job and taking another, and they will have no particular incentive to remain where they are. For the employer, this is a costly prospect. New workers must be trained at some expense, and initially they are likely to be less productive than veteran employees, driving up labor costs per unit of output. A company can reduce the turnover problem by offering wages above the market-clearing level. However, there is often no good way to identify in advance those workers who are most likely to switch jobs and pay them enough to avoid turnover without also paying a higher wage to many workers who have no plans to leave. Workers then face the possibility of finding lower wages or even unemployment if they venture back into the pool of the unemployed. Those consequences may make workers less inclined to leave, reducing employee turnover and thus lowering unit costs. But once again, the social impact of these higher wage levels will be seen in a lower level of unemployment.

There are also psychological reasons for paying a relatively high wage and treating workers in ways that local standards perceive to be "fair." Motivation of employees, after all, is a critical problem for almost all managers. "Fair" treatment may help develop a loyalty among workers that redounds to the firm's financial benefit. Costly job switches will become less frequent. Misbehavior is less of a problem, because workers are likely to reciprocate the employer's generosity by performing their work conscientiously. These effects reduce the employer's total costs, so paying a high wage becomes efficient for the firm—but, because wages are higher than in a free market equilibrium, the employer hires fewer workers than he or she otherwise would. Again, society experiences unemployment as a result.[12]

These models, like all economic models, are abstractions, and no single one of them is likely to explain completely the persistence of unemployment in modern economies. But looking inside the employment relationship, rather than at overarching social or economic factors, does seem to shed light on at least part of the structure of labor markets in the United States.

According to recent studies of wages in the United States, workers in many industries and occupations earn more than would be expected after taking age, sex, education, experience, union status, and other factors into consideration. Although free market economic theories predict that these high wages should fall over time to market-clearing levels as employers alter their wage offers and workers adjust their expectations, economists Alan B. Krueger and Lawrence H. Summers have found no evidence that wages do adjust in that way; on the contrary, they argue that the unexpected disparities among wages paid in different industries have persisted over at least half a century and are visible in a number of different countries. Their analysis of data from government population surveys in the United States indicates that the higher a worker's premium above the basic market-clearing wage, the less likely that worker is to leave his job, just as efficiency wage theories suggest. In addition, workers receiving higher wage premiums are more likely to report that their work is "meaningful" to them, that they think about it during their leisure time, and that it does not entail constant repetition—all signs that higher wages are associated with jobs that are difficult to monitor and that these higher wages are effective in inducing workers to perform with relatively little supervision. That result, as well, is what efficiency wage theories would predict.[13]

There is also evidence that the need to maintain a favorable public image makes it unprofitable for employers to adjust wages constantly in the face of changes in labor supply and demand, as they would have to were unemployment to be self-correcting. Surveys performed in Canada show the public does not regard it as "fair" for a firm to reduce workers' take-home pay simply because other workers willing to work for less are available. The public considers pay cuts to be legitimate only if the firm is losing money or is threatened by bankruptcy. Under other circumstances, a company that cuts workers' pay to market-clearing levels may well harm its reputation among customers, public officials, and potential employees, which could cost it more in the long run than it would save with lower wages.[14]

After comparing wages in various industries, William T. Dickens and Lawrence Katz found large and persistent differentials in pay that could not be readily explained as the workings of a competitive labor market. Both economic factors such as the difficulty of monitoring workers and sociological factors such as understandings of fairness lead employers frequently to pay wages above market-clearing levels, they concluded, lending general support to the efficiency wage hypothesis. But one major puzzle remains: these interindustry differences are similar across occupations, although it is not apparent why, say, a secretary in an auto plant should earn more than a secretary in an insurance office. That discrepancy suggests that the implications of efficiency wage theory are still not fully understood.[15]

But it is clear that the theory of efficiency wages explains at least some real-world decisions about workers' pay, and therefore the aggregate amount of employment and unemployment in an economy, better than traditional free market models with highly flexible wages. With efficiency wages, some workers in a society may have to endure involuntary unemployment due to no fault of their own but to individual employers' decisions to pay high wages to others. Efficiency wage theory also clarifies employers' reasons for laying off workers at times of insufficient work rather than reducing working hours across the board: the latter measure would reduce the incomes of more productive and less productive workers in equal degree, leading the more productive to seek alternative employment and leaving the firm with a lower-quality work force.

The unemployment attributable to efficiency wages will not disappear by itself. Some workers may be unable to locate employment through no fault of their own. But the standard array of economic policies advocated by believers in small government will do little to help them. The monetarist program of government actions to stabilize the inflation rate will have no effect on employers' individual decisions to pay high wages. Unions and minimum wage laws are not the cause of efficiency wages, so weakening their power is of little import in the overall employment picture. Helping workers and employers become more aware of the true market-clearing wage, as rational expectations theory would suggest, is also useless, since misperceptions about wage levels are not at the heart of the economic problem; on the contrary, workers and employers have *deliberately* chosen to agree on wages that are above the market-clearing level.

If the cures of political conservatism are irrelevant, the approaches traditionally favored by political liberals seem equally unhelpful in eliminating unemployment. Driving the economy faster by printing money or cutting taxes will have only temporary effects as a burst of inflation drives down real wages, since employers themselves will seek to restore wages to their earlier value as quickly as possible. The traditional spending programs of the welfare state would also prove counterproductive. A large-scale government-sponsored job creation program, for example, would reduce the potential costs of unemployment to workers, leading to more shirking on the job and hence to lower productivity. If employers seek to maintain worker discipline by raising their wage offers even higher, unemployment will be made worse, not better.

Efficiency wage theories, then, offer a challenge to political leaders and government administrators. The case for some form of government intervention in the labor market is clear enough, because the individual decisions of thousands of employers to pay high wages, while efficient for them, collectively cause major inefficiencies for society. Workers who could otherwise be productive are left jobless, and the economy's total output is far less than it could be. By simply letting the private market act, the government would be ignoring the social spillovers of all of these private actions and acquiescing in permanent unemployment. But the traditional measures put forth by economists offer little hope of dealing with the problem. What's needed is a new approach, attacking the structures of individual employment relationships rather than focusing on broad economic factors. If employers cause unemployment by paying excessive wages because of lack of information, lack of other employee performance incentives, the difficulty of monitoring workers, or the desire to maintain a reputation for "fairness," the only way to reduce the unemployment rate is to address those problems.

Some of the possible ways to do so lack appeal. One extreme approach would be to tax the unemployed. If every jobless person had to pay a special tax, workers would have strong incentives not to lose their jobs. Employers would not need to depend on wages to maintain their efficiency, so they could reduce their wage premiums and would hire more workers at lower pay. Overall, the rate of unemployment would probably fall and output would rise, assuming, of course, that the government actually had the determination to enforce the tax law against people without a source of income with which to pay. But unless wages were to fall all the way to the market-clearing level, unemployment would not disappear altogether—and those unfortunate enough to remain unemployed would be far worse off than they are now, having to draw on their depleted resources to pay a punishing tax.

A less punitive and far more positive alternative would be a government subsidy of wages. Employers would pay something close to the market-clearing wage from their own pockets, and the government would chip in an additional amount. This high level of pay would give workers the motivation to work hard to retain their jobs, while the employer would have an incentive to hire more workers than he or she has now. The subsidy would have to be small enough, however, that employers would not want to hire every last person seeking work, since a total absence of long-term unemployment would remove the penalty for workers who shirk. In the best of all worlds, the subsidies would be used to encourage the creation of jobs for which the market-clearing wage is already relatively high and not those for which wages are low, since high-wage jobs create more economic wealth.[16]

The government could also address the information problems that cause employers to pay above-market wages. For example, since employers are reluctant to cut paychecks because the best workers will identify themselves by leaving, the government could increase wage flexibility by making it easier for employers to identify which are the better workers, enabling firms to tailor wages more closely to workers' individual abilities and productivity. In this context, privacy laws barring disclosure of information related to job performance, restrictions on aptitude testing of job applicants, and court decisions that discourage former employers from offering frank references are bad policy, because they make it harder for companies to obtain high-quality information about their workers. If employers had better information, the gap between actual wages and the market-clearing wages for workers of varying abilities could be reduced, allowing companies to increase their total hiring and thus bringing down unemployment.

Reducing the cost of labor turnover to employers is one frequently mentioned way to help lower the unemployment rate, on the assumption that employers would then feel less need to pay above-market wages to retain workers. One way would be for the government to subsidize the expense of recruiting new employees, either through direct grants or by expanding existing job placement offices. Another would be to subsidize training costs, to minimize the cost of replacing an experienced worker who leaves. In either case, employers might be able to reduce the wage premium they pay to discourage turnover and would therefore be likely to put more workers on the job. Paradoxically, however, making it too easy for workers to move from one job to another might be counterproductive, because that would reduce the search costs of employees who are considering switching jobs and encourage them to embark on a job search they might not undertake if they had to bear the expense themselves. Some employers might then find it necessary to raise the wage premiums they pay to keep their workers from jumping ship, which, as we have seen, would lead to more rather than less unemployment.[17] As in so many other areas of economic behavior, employment grants and subsidies can have unintended effects unless they are used with care.

All of these ideas raise an obvious objection. The policies suggested by efficiency wage models involve reducing the pay workers actually receive to levels closer to the market-clearing wage. In the process, income would be redistributed from those workers who are currently employed at high wages to workers who currently have no employment at all. Many advocates of government action to alleviate unemployment, including both traditional political liberals and Marxists, would argue for forcing employers to bear part of the cost. The only way to do this consistent with the efficiency wage models presented here is to require employers to hire more workers without reducing the compensation of those already on board. But this would reduce firms' efficiency both by drastically slashing the ratio of capital to labor and by putting less productive workers on the job. The net result for the economy would not be positive.

Efficiency wage models do not lend support to the cherished political goal of full employment. On the contrary, they indicate that if unemployment were somehow totally abolished, the worker incentive problems described earlier would make for a sharp decline in economic efficiency. Reducing unemployment to a low level will make the entire economy better off, but eliminating it altogether will make the economy less, not more, productive. For society as a whole, unpleasant as the prospect may be, the economy will perform at its utmost if there are always some people out of work. No one is yet in a position to guess how low this socially optimal level of unemployment is, although there is little doubt that it is far below the persistently high unemployment rates of recent years.

Efficiency wage theories represent a new direction in economic activism. They do not vanquish the arguments for using monetary and fiscal policies to deal with large cyclical fluctuations in unemployment or with joblessness caused by sudden changes in the world economy. Cutting taxes, boosting spending, or printing money may have broad macroeconomic uses that efficiency wage theories do not deal with, and they are certainly important in affecting the distribution of income to ensure that the costs of being unemployed are spread widely within the economy, rather than being borne consistently by a small number of workers or by certain ethnic groups. But efficiency wage theories tell us that in a world in which incentives matter, in which people lack information and are unable to protect against all risks, there are limits to what government policy can achieve. Attempting to eliminate long-term unemployment totally would be socially undesirable. Leaving unemployment to the free market would be equally destructive. A modest effort to alleviate the factors that keep people from obtaining jobs may be the best that government can do.

5
We're All Monetarists Now

In the controversy over government's ability to shape the course of economic events, no question is more important than this: Does money matter? Through its powers to create money, to pull money out of circulation, and, by regulating bank reserves, to control the extent to which that money is recycled within the economy, the government can alter monetary policy almost instantaneously. The issue long debated by economists is whether this policy tool can be used to increase the amount of goods and services the economy produces, or whether it does nothing but change the prices charged for those goods and services while leaving the quantity of output unchanged. One of the most surprising developments of modern economics is that theorists and empirical analysts alike are moving toward a general consensus about what monetary policy can do—and about what it cannot do.

Through most of human history, societies have used as their medium of exchange some commodity that would be valued even were it not used as money: cattle, foodstuffs, decorative objects, metals. Even where a government minted coins, the value of those coins was nothing more than the value of the precious metal they contained. Under those circumstances, government could do little to control the money supply. Many governments chose to base their money on gold, a relatively scarce mineral, because the lack of gold would put an automatic limit on the amount of money in circulation—until the discovery of a new mine suddenly increased the supply of gold and, by giving people more money to buy goods without adding to the amount of goods available for purchase, drove up prices. When the money supply depended directly upon the amount of some commodity, "monetary policy" as we know it today was not an issue except in selecting the commodity to be used. The nineteenth-century arguments over whether the money supply should be based upon gold alone or also upon silver, which is much more plentiful, took the place of modern debates over whether the money supply is growing too fast. The political import of both debates is the same: just as increasing the money supply causes inflation and thus favors people who owe fixed amounts of currency over the people who lent them the money, basing the currency on a faster-growing supply of silver favored debtors over creditors, who naturally preferred "hard money" tied to a relatively stable supply of gold.

Deliberate government control of the supply of money as that concept is understood today, then, is an issue only in an economy in which the amount of money in circulation is not directly limited by the supply of some commodity. That describes most major economies today, in which the value of money is determined strictly by the demand and supply for money itself: if the supply of dollars or marks or pounds goes up faster than the demand, each unit of currency will lose value in terms of "real" goods like bread and gasoline and airplane rides. The result, of course, is inflation and with it a loss of confidence in the country's economy. Conversely, an increase in the supply of money smaller than the growth in demand leads to deflation, a situation that can bring about a cascading economic collapse when debtors find that the real value of their debts is far larger than they anticipated and their inability to pay brings their creditors down with them.

The existence of some relationship between money supply growth and price changes is acknowledged by almost all economists working today. All other things being equal, managing the money supply to keep prices stable seems a worthwhile goal. But are all other things equal? This has become one of the central controversies of economic policy: Do changes in the money supply affect only the level of prices, or do they also have an effect on the "real" side of the economy, where people are employed and goods and services are produced? Can monetary policy be used to speed up or slow down the rate of economic growth?

Until the past few decades, that subject seemed relatively peripheral to the debate over whether, and in what way, the government can foster economic growth. Many people of course observed that interest rates that are low relative to the rate of inflation make it more attractive for people and businesses to hold cash and to borrow money for investment, while high real interest rates tend to choke off investment-dependent sectors of the economy, such as housing and capital goods. Keynes himself implied that monetary policy could stimulate the economy by undermining the reluctance of workers and business people to lower their wage and price demands in a slack economy: inflation could overcome this price stickiness by reducing the real value of wages and prices, helping the economy achieve a more efficient allocation of resources.

But for Keynes, and for most economic policy makers from the 1930s to the 1960s, these effects seemed relatively minor. Many of them believed that the money supply accommodates itself to spending, rather than the other way around, making monetary growth an unimportant variable in the economic equation. The new science of demand management, involving manipulation of public spending and taxation, was thought to be a far more powerful force in shaping economic growth.

The first systematic challenge to the view that monetary policy is of secondary importance did not come until 1960, with the publication of Milton Friedman's *Program for Monetary Stability*, followed three years later by Friedman's and Anna Schwartz's classic *Monetary History of the United States*. The trouble with government economic policy over the preceding century, Friedman and Schwartz argued, was not that the government had failed to manage its spending and taxation in response to the state of the economy. Rather, they said, erratic monetary policy was the problem. While the public's demand for money seemed remarkably stable, growing only at a very slow rate, changes in the money supply had often been swift and unpredictable. These money supply changes correlated with booms and depressions, indicating that monetary policy, whether deliberate or inadvertent, was far more important to the economy than most Keynesians had assumed. As Friedman put it, "Money matters." But while changes in the stock of money have only a short-term impact on economic growth, he argued, they leave a residue of inflation that persists long after the effects on output and unemployment have come and gone.[1]

This analysis led to a startling conclusion: if the demand for money is in fact nearly stable, the central bank should keep the supply of money nearly stable as well, allowing it to increase only in tandem with demand. This would benefit the economy by eliminating inflation, creating an environment conducive to long-term economic growth. Of course tying money supply growth to money demand means that increases in the money supply cannot be used as a shot of stimulus during economic downturns. But in the Friedman-Schwartz view, that is no disadvantage, since the benefits of such a policy would be purely transitory, while the costs in terms of inflation will be long-lasting.

The assertion that "money matters" was a strong and valid critique of the Keynesian ideas that dominated government policy both in the United States and Britain during the 1960s. But Friedman went even further, arguing that nothing but money matters in the long run. Expansionary fiscal policy, he conceded, may result in higher output, but only for a brief period of time before rising prices bring an end to the boom. Tax policy too may increase output but only by reducing economic disincentives to work or invest, not—as Keynesians would believe—by reducing the tax take so more money is available for spending. Because of these inherent limitations of fiscal measures, government should give up trying to use budget and tax policies for macroeconomic objectives such as reducing the unemployment rate or stimulating business investment. In 1968 Karl Brunner, an economist with beliefs similar to Friedman's, termed their approach *monetarism*, setting it in deliberate apposition to the *fiscalism* that then dominated economic thinking.

To translate their philosophy into economic policy, the monetarists persuaded major central banks to make a basic change in the way they ran their affairs. Central bankers had traditionally tried to discern whether monetary policy was too loose or too tight by watching interest rates or employment statistics. If a key rate was below the level the government desired or if low unemployment and high wage increases indicated incipient inflation, the central bank would typically try to raise the interest rate it charged to commercial banks or would sell government bonds, soaking up excess cash. The monetarists, however, argued that by responding to these changes in the "real" economy, central bankers actually ended up increasing, rather than minimizing, fluctuations in employment, production, and prices. They advised the banks instead to gear their operations to artificial targets, labeled monetary aggregates, which measure the amount of money in circulation according to different definitions: one counts only cash and immediate substitutes for cash, such as travelers' checks and checking account balances, while others include savings accounts and other deposits that are likely to be spent less readily.

These aggregates have no intrinsic importance, but monetarists argued that they are useful targets because they have a stable relationship to economic performance. Central banks cannot control them directly. The monetarist teaching, however, was that a government or its central bank should determine in advance how fast the demand for money will grow and then keep the aggregates growing steadily at that same rate. If the targets were set properly, that policy would result in noninflationary economic growth.

Monetarists made no claims that following their monetary rule would lead to full employment at all times. Full employment, Friedman contended, was beyond the power of government macroeconomic policies to achieve. Each economy, he argued, has a "natural" rate of unemployment, the lowest rate that can be maintained over the long run given the structure of the economy. Active government policy, such as an increase in spending or in the supply of money, might temporarily reduce unemployment below that natural rate by causing inflation that would reduce the real value of wages. Once everyone realizes the extent of inflation, however, they will adjust their wage and price demands accordingly, returning unemployment to its natural level but leaving continuing inflation. Conversely, in an inflationary economy noninflationary monetary growth may lead to a temporary increase in unemployment, but as soon as workers and employers realize that prices are no longer escalating and adjust their inflation expectations accordingly, unemployment will again fall to the natural rate. Monetary policy, then, has no effect on unemployment except in the very short term. All it can do is keep prices stable, eliminating the inflationary worries and uncertainties that can distract people from engaging in economically productive activities.[2]

The monetarist story relied on two critical assumptions about the role of money in the economy. The first was that the velocity of money—that rate at which money changes hands—would continue to increase at about 3 percent per year, a trend it had followed closely since 1953. The second was that the demand for money was almost insensitive to interest rates, so that the Federal Reserve could follow the same money growth path whether interest rates were high or low. The latter assumption also implied that "real" economic events that might affect interest rates, such as a bad harvest, a cut in federal spending, or the invention of a new labor-saving technology, would have no impact on the demand for money, so the Fed could safely ignore them in formulating its policies.

Keynesians objected to Friedman's approach, arguing that the concept of "money" is so vague it cannot be controlled according to a simple rule. But the first strong theoretical attack on monetarism came from the rational expectationists. The monetarist story, they protested, assumes that monetary policy has short-term effects on unemployment because workers and employers are slow to comprehend the fact that the inflation rate is changing. But if individuals' expectations are truly rational, there will be a time lag only in comprehending *unanticipated* policy changes. When a new rate of money supply growth is announced in advance and then followed, people will incorporate that announced change into their expectations even before it actually occurs, negating its effects. If everyone understands in advance that the Fed intends to tighten the money supply, there will be no effect at all on employment or output when the new policy takes effect, because individuals have already anticipated the change and reduced their wage and interest rate demands to a noninflationary level. Money is neutral, unable to affect the economy in any systematic way.[3]

The addition of rational expectations principles thus led to a dangerous change in the public's understanding of monetarism. Where the original monetarists, such as Friedman and Brunner, warned that antiinflationary monetary policies would be painful until the economy adjusted, the rational expectationists suggested that simply announcing a slower rate of money supply growth would cure inflation almost painlessly. Workers would immediately lower their wage demands. Interest rates would fall as lenders stopped charging premiums to cover expected inflation. The political appeal of such a message was obvious. In Britain, in Canada, and in the United States, where central banks had publicly abandoned interest rate targeting in favor of monetary aggregates, politicians promised to make a quick end to inflation without the recessions that had historically gone hand in hand with tight money. Supply-siders too grabbed onto the new monetarism, which offered a way to make their promises of painless economic adjustment intellectually respectable.

What happened, of course, was nothing of the sort. Despite ample warnings of tight money and publication of low targets for growth in the monetary aggregates, sharply deflationary monetary policies starting in the late 1970s threw all three economies into tailspins. Workers' wage demands and investors' interest rate expectations came down far more slowly than the inflation rate itself, belying rational expectationists' assertion that adjustment would be almost instantaneous. Although many monetarists sharply criticized the U.S. Federal Reserve Board for failing to maintain the growth of monetary aggregates within a narrow target range, the Fed rightly saw that exceptionally tight money was required in 1982 to counterbalance the inflationary effects of an unprecedented budget deficit, and that loosening the reins thereafter was necessary to allow the lower interest rates essential to the U.S. economy's recovery from the deepest depression since the 1930s. Rational expectations theory notwithstanding, monetary policy did appear to have real—and sometimes painful—effects on the economy. Attempting to stabilize the monetary aggregates proved not to be helpful in stabilizing employment or output and actually led to greater instability of interest rates.[4] The central bank was forced to divert from its intended course.

The events of the 1980s thus cast serious doubt on the monetarist recipe for inflation-free prosperity. But paradoxically, even as the purported benefits of mandating a fixed rate of growth of the monetary aggregates have disappeared, economists have increasingly come to agree with one firm monetarist premise: rules, rather than total discretion, are needed to guide the hand of the central bank.

The virtue of rules to guide monetary policy is a surprising point of convergence for economic thinkers in the 1980s. Throughout the 1970s, debates over monetary policy had two major sides, one demanding a firm standard to govern the growth of the monetary aggregates, the other emphasizing the need for central bankers to exercise discretion in shaping monetary policy. A decade later, those firm and time-tested battle lines are nowhere to be found. With the monetarist contention that money is an extremely potent tool now widely accepted, nonmonetarist economists have increasingly devoted their attention to considering how the money supply should be managed. They have generally accepted the view that unpredictable monetary policy sows needless and even harmful confusion in the economy. In addition, it is clear that the political systems in democratic countries have a tendency to create inflation, as politicians seek to maximize short-term economic output in order to please political constituencies. Monetary policy rules provide a useful means of countering such pressures and making the government's commitment to fight inflation credible. Economic controversy no longer centers on whether there should be rules to govern the creation of money but rather on what those rules should be— and on how much discretion the central bank should be allowed to exercise when it believes that the rules are not achieving their purpose.

The monetarists' money supply rules were based on the presumption that the demand for money could be predicted and the supply tailored accordingly. But the demand for money turns out to be unpredictable, while the concept of the "money supply" has proved to be far more slippery than monetarists foresaw. Both of these problems came into evidence in the early 1980s, following the decision by the Federal Reserve Board in October 1979 to make steady growth of the monetary aggregates its monetary policy goal, rather than worrying directly about interest rates.

The major focus of Fed attention was M1, the aggregate that includes balances of cash and near-cash. M1 was widely felt to be the most important aggregate, because unlike the savings accounts contained in M2 and the time deposits in M3, the balances in M1 could immediately be used for consumer or business spending. Each Thursday afternoon, the business world waited nervously for the release of the latest money supply report from the Federal Reserve Bank of New York, the numbers that would reveal whether M1 was above, below, or within the targeted path. But even as the economy hung ever more carefully on each movement in the growth path of

M1, the relationship between M1 and the economy was changing. Investment advisory companies began offering money market funds, which paid investors higher interest than bank deposits and included check-writing privileges. Balances in those accounts, however, were included only in M2, not in M1. Then federal banking regulators allowed financial institutions to offer interest-bearing accounts with negotiable orders of withdrawal—a long way of saying "checks." These accounts were technically savings accounts, so they were included in M2. But checks drawn on them could be used to buy cars and television sets, just like checks drawn on the non-interest-bearing accounts in M1. Although the Fed retained the ability to control M1, that ceased to be a useful proxy for "money."

That same fundamental problem applies to the other monetary aggregates as well. The creativity of financial entrepreneurs in devising new types of accounts and investment vehicles and the effects of technological changes in altering the speed with which money can move from one account to another indicate that the relationships between the aggregates and the economy are unstable at best. A central bank that runs monetary policy to hit a target level of M1 or M2 will be forced to readjust those targets continually in light of new evidence about how a change in the aggregates affects output, employment, prices, or interest rates. But allowing it to do so grants the central bank that very power that monetarists sought to deprive it of: discretion in determining monetary policy.

Similar uncertainties arose on the demand side. The demand for money proved to be highly responsive to "real" factors in the economy, contrary to the monetarist prediction. Higher interest rates led to a sharp drop in the demand for money. Because the costs to individuals of simply holding cash are high when those funds could earn high interest rates instead, the velocity of money rises sharply during periods of high rates rather than remaining stable. Real factors that affected interest rates during the early 1980s, such as the Organization of Petroleum Exporting Countries' oil boycott of 1979 and the major tax law changes in the United States in 1981, thus led to major changes in money demand. A central bank monetary policy that ignored these economic disturbances and focused solely on the monetary aggregates in an effort to bring inflation down, as monetarists advised, could not avoid driving the economy into recession, because the underlying assumption that demand for money will remain stable while the supply is scaled back is not valid.

Finding an alternative to the monetarists' simple but unsound rule, however, has proved a troublesome undertaking. For all its problems, a rule targeting monetary aggregates has simple virtues: the amount of M1 or M2 in circulation can be determined with great precision, and the current week's value can be computed within a few days after the week is over. Save interest rates, the same can be said for very few other important economic data. Many neoclassical economists opposed to active government intervention in the economy, including most monetarists, argue for using a monetary rule despite its acknowledged imperfections. At least, they say, it will bar the path to inflation. "What alternative theory is there?" asks Allan Meltzer, one of the leading monetarist scholars. "If monetarist theory has done so badly, what theory has done better?"[5]

But the argument that a plainly unsatisfactory rule should be adopted simply because no more proven rule is available is hardly convincing. A bad rule could cause serious economic harm. Had it remained firmly in place in the United States after 1982, the monetarist rule would undoubtedly have kept the economy in depression, rather than allowing a strong burst of economic growth. William Poole, a monetarist who served on the Council of Economic Advisers from 1982 to 1983, argues that the experience of the 1980s demonstrates that a firm monetary growth rule may function well in times of economic stability but is not the best way to manage the money supply during the transition from high inflation to low inflation. And, Poole cautions, "there is no formula to determine when the transition should terminate."[6] Translation: no one can know when is the proper time to put the monetary rule into effect, so the central bank will have to use its discretion.

Many economists, including Herbert Stein, an influential adviser to several Republican presidents, have advocated that the Federal Reserve target a specific rate of growth of the gross national product each year. Using that target and a prediction about the velocity of money, the Fed would know how fast the money supply should grow, Stein asserts.[7] But quite aside from the difficulty of

predicting velocity—Stein would allow the Fed to change its estimate in response to "strong evidence" that velocity has changed—
the first GNP estimate for the current three-month period is not
published until six weeks after the quarter ends, and the figure tends
to be inaccurate for several months until additional data become
available. It may be July before the Fed can know whether the monetary policy it pursued in January achieved the desired rate of GNP
growth. The current-dollar value of GNP, then, is difficult to use
for purposes of monetary targeting. So are other frequently mentioned variables, such as real (inflation-adjusted) output, gross domestic product, and final consumer demand.

Interest rates too are a troublesome target for monetary policy.
Nominal rates, the percentages that borrowers pay in interest, are
easy to determine. Whether the prime rate is at 6 percent or 9 percent, however, is not necessarily a matter of great economic importance. What is important is the spread between the prime and the
anticipated rate of inflation, the "real" interest rate. But the real rate
is far more uncertain than the nominal rate, because it depends
upon how, and over what time period, investors' expectations of
inflation are defined. In addition, of course, the real rate may be
different for each taxpayer, because the after-tax return varies according to how the tax laws affect the transaction. And real rates
can sometimes obscure economic changes: if interest rates and inflation rates rise in tandem, the real rate will be unchanged, yet
there are clearly other economic changes afoot that are causing inflation to rise.

Yet another possible rule for monetary policy involves stabilizing prices, whether through a general price index, an exchange rate,
or prices of gold or other specific commodities. The central bank
could establish the relevant price index, declare its present value to
equal 100, and make it the goal of monetary policy to keep the
index at 100 in the future.[8] Supply-siders, in particular, make the
case for a rule featuring a commodity price index. Movements in
commodity prices, they contend, are precursors of inflation elsewhere in the economy. Stabilizing the price index, then, would result
in the general stabilization of prices.

But this simple-sounding rule has its disadvantages too. A central bank has no tools that directly affect prices, unless it wants to

get into the business of buying, selling, and stockpiling commodities. The monetary policy tools it does have affect prices with a lag that is far more variable than the six-to-nine-month period economists once took for granted. A rapid price rise now does not reflect this week's monetary policy but rather the policy in effect in months past. If prices are rising this month, the central bank has no way of knowing whether its actions of the past several months will eventually stem inflation or whether further monetary tightening is needed. If it tightens unnecessarily, of course, it could be pushing the economy into recession to deal with an inflation problem that was already on the way to being resolved. A firm rule dictating the maintenance of a specific price level is more likely to destabilize than stabilize the economy.

Nor does such a price rule dispense with the discretion of central bankers. Someone must determine which commodities should be in the index. Should its composition be changed if some of its components—copper, for example, or iron—lose their economic importance due to the development of substitute products? And what if the index should rise or fall due not to changes in domestic demand but to one-time supply shocks, such as a freeze in Brazil's coffee-producing regions or the discovery of a major new oil field? The perceptions of the individuals in charge of monetary policy will be vital in deciding what course to pursue.[9]

All of the possible alternatives to the monetarist rule governing money supply growth, then, present problems of their own. None of them can provide the basis for a mechanistic monetary policy leaving no room for human discretion. Economists of all points of view have come to recognize that a policy that cannot be departed from is inadvisable. The changing relationships between the tools a central bank has at its disposal and the economy they are supposed to affect mean that any mechanistic rule will need constant adjustment if it is not to lead to undesired results. A central bank must be prepared to change its course in response to economic shocks, to government tax and budget decisions, and to the decisions of foreign central banks that could affect exchange rates. At best, a monetary rule can serve as a general principle from which policymakers depart only after serious deliberation and, perhaps, after formal notice to the public. The pressing question is whether a central bank can systematically use such departures to put the economy on a course of higher output or lower unemployment.

The assertion that a central bank's manipulation of the money supply will alter only prices, not output or employment, rests upon fragile economic assumptions. Those are the standard assumptions of classical economics: perfect markets, perfect information, perfectly rational individual actors, perfect capital markets, and, of course, a tax system that imposes only some mythical nondistorting tax upon the citizenry. If the money supply increases in this economically perfect world, individuals will use their excess cash to bid up the prices of goods and services until, at the end, everything costs more in terms of dollars or pounds or marks but the relative prices of various goods are unchanged. Once those price adjustments have occurred, employment and output will return to their previous levels.

But if the economy features imperfect competition, including monopolies or near-monopolies in the production of certain products, the results of monetary policy may be very different. The costs individual firms would incur in adjusting to a change in the money supply (called "menu costs" after the cost of printing new menus to reflect price changes) might inhibit them from changing prices instantaneously if the changes would be small. Under perfect competition, that is no problem: business will automatically flow to the firm with the lowest prices, and others will be forced to make the price change if they wish to compete. Total economic output will be the same. In the more monopolistic environment of a modern industrial economy, however, firms are normally able to reduce output and raise prices beyond what perfect competition would allow. If the costs of raising prices lead the monopolist not to adjust prices each time there is a small increase in the money supply, customers will demand more of the monopolist's product and the monopolist will have to produce more in order to maximize profits. That higher production makes the economy better off. For each individual firm, the effects of these minor deviations from the prior pattern of production are unimportant. For the economy as a whole, however, if many firms temporarily increase their output rather than raising prices each time the money supply goes up, monetary policy may prove to be a significant tool for increasing economic output.[10]

Imperfect information too may give monetary policy a potency it would not have in an economically perfect world. If the central bank decides to tighten the money supply, it typically does that by selling bonds in the open market, draining off funds that were previously being put to some other purpose. As banks reduce their reserves in order to buy the bonds, they are forced to reduce the amount of loans they have outstanding, since the loans must legally be backed by reserves. But raising interest rates for everyone is not the best way for the bank to scale back its lending, because that would increase some borrowers' probabilities of default more than others'. Instead, a bank short on funds is likely to cut off some borrowers altogether to maintain its favored customers. Those borrowers will have difficulty obtaining credit elsewhere, because the fact that their banks have cut them off serves as a black mark against them with other lenders, who lack perfect information about the borrowers' creditworthiness. The result will be that favored customers will always be able to borrow, while other customers, particularly those viewed as having higher risks, will be unable to obtain credit when money is tight. In such a case, monetary policy does far more than raise nominal interest rates for everyone. It directly affects economic performance by making it harder for some firms to obtain credit than for others, changing the mix of production.[11]

And what if individuals are not perfectly rational? Suppose that people and companies adjust their wage and price demands to money supply changes quickly but not instantaneously. Economists would call them "near rational" because they fall slightly short of maximizing their economic welfare. When the central bank increases the money supply, a near-rational firm won't immediately raise prices. Demand for the firm's products will increase, and the company may actually need to hire more workers, if it can find near-rational workers who have not increased their own wage demands. For the firms and individuals concerned, the loss in welfare from this nonrationality may be trivial. But, surprisingly, if this behavior is repeated by thousands of firms throughout an economy, the result may be a major increase in employment at the cost of only a tiny reduction in the firms' profits. Monetary policy in such a near-rational world can have extremely powerful effects on the real economy. It is anything but "neutral."[12]

As a result of these findings, monetary policy finds itself in a very confused state in the late 1980s. There are no simple rules that tell a central bank when to tighten or loosen the money supply, no easy guides to action. There is wide agreement that formal monetary rules are desirable for both economic and political reasons, but every attempt to devise rules—save a rule that focuses on maintaining the value of a currency in terms of some other currency, putting the nation completely at the mercy of some other nation's economic policies—has faltered. Rules may be useful as guideposts, or as standards from which the monetary authorities should not deviate without conscious decision, but not, at least given the current state of knowledge, as rigid and unalterable constraints.

The idea of putting monetary policy on autopilot remains attractive to many political conservatives, with their instinctive distrust of having human beings make arbitrary decisions that affect the economic activities of others. But there is no indication that economists are drawing any closer to finding the magic money supply rule. Implicit in the calls for adopting some rule now despite this relative ignorance is the assumption that government authorities cannot successfully use monetary policy as an active tool of economic management, an assumption that has been sharply challenged by recent research. Money really does matter in shaping the course of economic growth. It is something that must be managed according to the wisdom and discretion of the central bankers whose job it is to understand and respond to the economic changes around them. In a world full of uncertainty and unpredictability, noninterventionist monetary policy is simply not a desirable option.

6

Inefficient Markets

As always, the telegram comes as a shock to the directors of Acme Corporation. J.Q. Moneyman, the famous Wall Street investor, has secretly bought 15 percent of Acme's stock over the past week, paying the market price of twenty dollars per share. Now, the telegram announces, Moneyman wants to buy the rest of the company's 10 million outstanding shares for twenty-seven dollars apiece.

A proposal like J.Q. Moneyman's raises a host of economic questions. Does the fact that the twenty-seven-dollar offer is above the current price mean that it is to the advantage of Acme's many owners, or might management's ten-year plan produce a better return over the long run? Did the people who unknowingly sold out for only twenty dollars get cheated because Moneyman was slow to announce his plans, or did they get a fair price? Will the buyout, financed by bonds, result in a more efficient company, or will the stream of future interest payments divert money that could be used far better to modernize factories and build research centers? If Acme's management buys the raider's shares back for twenty-five dollars each, are the company's other owners being treated unfairly? Will some of these investors, angry at their treatment, quit the market altogether, making it harder for all corporations to sell stock?

The answers to all of these questions depend critically on yet another question that affects almost everyone, one that economists have been studying intensely: How well do the financial markets work?

Strong, privately run markets have played a critical role in the rapid economic growth of the market economies of North America, Europe, and Japan. Highly liquid, well-publicized stock and bond markets make it easy and inexpensive for corporations to raise money for plants and equipment, for governments to finance their deficits, and for families to purchase homes and automobiles. Millions of individuals increase their wealth by using the impersonal market to make their savings available to entrepreneurs they have never met, who will use their funds to establish or expand their businesses. Insurance and futures markets provide an organized way for people to share risk, so an unexpected change in exchange rates or commodity prices, a sudden illness or a natural disaster will not destroy a business or impoverish a family. Even individuals who put their cash in a mattress rather than investing it on Wall Street cannot remain aloof: by virtue of participating in pension funds, mutual insurance companies, or neighborhood credit unions, they too are inextricably bound up in the world of international finance.

Among economists, financial markets have traditionally been treated with suspicion. Far more than the markets for avocados or appliances, financial markets are thought to generate irrational psychological behavior. Time after time, frenzied investors eager to get rich quick have bid up the price of some asset or other far higher than any reasonable expectation of return would justify, only to see their speculative bubbles collapse. At times, such events have dragged entire economies into depression, costing millions of people their life's savings.[1] The economic consequences of past financial market crises were so traumatic that almost all governments now seek actively to prevent them from recurring. "It is usually agreed that casinos should, in the public interest, be inaccessible and expensive," noted John Maynard Keynes. "And perhaps the same is true of stock exchanges."[2] Such sentiments have led to bank deposit insurance, regulation of securities issuers and dealers, and requirements that insurance companies maintain sound financial reserves of a specified size in order to pay their claims.

But many of the government's efforts to oversee markets have come under sharp attack from advocates of unrestrained competition. Left to themselves, these believers in small government argue, markets will operate efficiently. Most forms of government intervention are alleged to interfere with this efficiency, keeping the markets from correctly determining prices and interest rates and making the economy worse off. Since its development began in the late

1960s, "efficient market theory" has been used by those who favor minimal government control of the stock, bond, and commodity futures markets, as well as of proponents of unregulated markets in foreign exchange.

Although its precise definition is mathematically complex, the basic meaning of market efficiency is simple: all known information relevant to a stock, a bond, or a futures contract is continuously incorporated into its price. Using their rational expectations, individuals will quickly and correctly determine how any piece of economic news will affect the performance of an investment, and they will immediately alter their offers to buy and sell so as to keep the security's price in line with their new expectations of the income it will generate. If people believe inflation is rising, the price of a bond will fall so that an investor purchasing it at its new, lower price will expect the same after-inflation return on each dollar invested as he or she would have given the previous price and previous expectations of inflation. If investors demand a much higher interest rate for a twenty-year bond than for a one-year bond, efficient market theory interprets the difference largely as an expectation that inflation in future years will be higher than it is at present.

Similarly, the price of General Motors Corporation common stock in an efficient market takes into account everything investors currently know about the company and its earnings prospects, the outlook for the auto industry, and the general state of the economy now and in the future. A drop of 1⅛ points in the price of GM's stock on the New York Stock Exchange this afternoon must indicate that investors have received new information leading them to attach less value to each GM share. For investors who don't follow GM's affairs closely, knowing the market price is sufficient for them to be fully informed about the company, on a par with every other investor. In its strongest form, efficient market theory contends that not even private information, such as a corporate president's knowledge of his own company's secret plans, will allow a person systematically to earn profits trading in the company's stock because others will observe the informed person's activities and bid up the price of the stock.

If efficient market theory is true, no one can consistently beat the market. On average, an investor will do as well to purchase securities and hold them as to trade actively in search of higher returns. Private research of the sort that many brokerage firms do is useless because the market offers no such thing as "undervalued" stocks that can be routinely identified and snapped up cheaply; every security is always fully valued, based on the information known at that time. Any trading strategy that temporarily outperforms the market will quickly be copied by others, eliminating the strategist's opportunity to profit at others' expense. Even professional money managers will be unable to do better than the market in general over a long period of time, so hiring a pro to pick stocks is hardly worth the trouble. One would do as well on average simply by purchasing a basket of stocks representative of the market as a whole.

That does not mean, of course, that investing will never be profitable. There are often lucky breaks. A particular investor may well strike it rich by correctly guessing that positive information in the future will sharply boost the value of a particular security. But in an efficient market such an extraordinary price increase is merely a random event, not a tribute to the investor's superior reasoning. In advance, there is no way to predict the arrival of good news. There is an equally good chance that bad news will cause the price to fall. After all, if there were a systematic way to identify those securities most likely to rise in price tomorrow, investors eager to buy them would drive up the price today. Earning unusually high returns on investment, efficient market theory proclaims, is strictly a matter of chance.

The term *efficient markets* is most often used in this private sense, relating to the gains and losses of individual investors. But the assertion that financial markets are completely efficient implies far more. If markets are fully efficient internally, eliminating systematic opportunities for profit, they must also be efficient externally, allocating capital in the way that will lead to the greatest economic growth.

The cause of this supposed social efficiency lies in the assumption that the return an investor receives reflects the productivity of his money as well as the risk involved. If one borrower is able to pay a higher interest rate than another and the risks to the lender are similar, the borrower able to pay more must intend to put the money to a more productive use, in which it will generate a greater income. An efficient market always assures that a borrower able to make more productive use of capital will be able to obtain it before a borrower who will use it less productively and therefore cannot afford to pay as much for it. So long as taxes do not interfere with this calculus by taking a greater share of the income from one type of investment than from another, money will be channeled systematically to the uses that produce the highest return for society.

This social efficiency, efficient market theorists contend, means that the returns in different financial markets are equalized. An investor buying one thousand dollars of Exxon Corporation common stock expects to earn the same total after-tax return, including dividends and changes in the value of the asset itself, as he or she would by placing one thousand dollars in any other investment entailing the same risk, be it Consolidated Edison Company bonds, wheat futures contracts, or options on the London Stock Exchange. When a company or a government comes to "the market" to raise money, the return it will have to offer investors must be at least as much as they can earn on other investments with similar risk characteristics. The riskiest projects, of course, should face the highest interest rates. Since those projects are also the ones that have the highest probability of producing no economic return for society at all, efficient financial markets effectively act as a filter, keeping would-be borrowers from using society's capital unless the potential returns are so large that the project's expected earnings justify the risk.

Efficient market theory has very strong implications for public policy. If markets are truly efficient, any government action that interferes with the market's assessment of risks and returns will reduce economic welfare. Corporate takeover attempts should not be regulated: a would-be acquirer willing to pay sixty-five dollars per share for a company previously selling for forty-five dollars must have some method of operating the company more profitably than current management can or he or she would not be able to offer such a premium. That more efficient operation will benefit society.[3] The use of high-risk "junk bonds" by companies already bearing heavy debt loads should be of no concern, as the high rate of interest investors demand to hold those bonds accurately reflects all of the risks involved. [4] Government programs to make sure that credit is available for certain purposes, such as the purchase of housing or the establishment of a small business, are undesirable because the market already directs the socially efficient amount of resources to those uses. At the extreme, some efficient market theorists even argue that the current legal prohibition against "insider" stock trading should be repealed, because in a totally efficient market inside information does not allow anyone to reap extra profits.

Efficient market theory thus fits neatly with other aspects of the laissez-faire philosophy of economics. As financial markets around the world grew rapidly in the 1980s, most governments adopted a hands-off attitude, even as the increasingly deregulated financial industry was undergoing traumatic changes and hundreds of new firms were fighting for a piece of the business. Bankers and investment bankers created a multitude of new financial instruments: bonds with special features that could change the return in midstream, swaps in which two companies exchange their obligations to pay interest on loans, packages of home mortgage or auto loans that can easily be dealt from one player to another. No one knew precisely how these instruments would perform during an economic slowdown or a period of high interest rates, but their growth was virtually unimpeded by government regulation. By correctly assessing risks and returns, it was assumed, the markets would sort things out.

In the United States, the unprecedented volatility of stock prices on Wall Street in 1986 and 1987[5] was of no concern to the government; such new developments as program trading, in which brokerage house computers triggered massive buy or sell orders based on the relative prices of stocks and stock options, destabilized the market, but the destabilization was attributed to the market's efficient workings. Leveraged buyouts, in which investors issued bonds to buy a publicly traded company from shareholders and operate it as a privately held corporation, proceeded unhindered, despite the puzzling fact that many companies purchased in this way were soon resold to the public for far more than shareholders had received just months earlier; these quick profits were attributed to superior management. Government-subsidized credit programs for students, farmers, owners of small businesses, and homebuyers were labeled as inefficient attempts to allocate credit and were scaled back. In the futures markets, the Commodity Futures Trading Commission permitted traders to conduct trades off the floor after hours, holding that private trading between two parties would not disadvantage other traders, since market efficiency meant the private trade would always occur at the free market price. Only the strong efforts by the Justice Department and the Securities and Exchange Commission to prosecute cases of alleged insider stock trading offered an indication that the most extreme dictum of the efficient market theorists was not fully accepted in Washington.

But although efficient market theory may have conquered the hearts and minds of those ideologically opposed to activist government, the notion that unrestrained markets operate efficiently has not passed the test of either empirical or theoretic scrutiny. Empirically, such events as the 508-point drop in the Dow Jones Industrial Average on October 19, 1987, are hard to square with the notion that markets are efficient. Believers in efficient markets face the burden of explaining what new information became available to investors on that day that caused them to value the stocks of the United States' leading corporations 22 percent less than they did the day before. And analyses of stock prices over the long term indicate that stocks that have fallen sharply are likely to rebound to their long-term average level, suggesting that investors often overreact when information indicating lower prices originally becomes available and are then slow to correct these mistakes, rather than operating with perfect rationality at all times—a tendency perhaps confirmed by the stock markets' near-record rise only two days after the October 19 crash.[6]

Theoretically, it turns out, a fully efficient market is an impossibility. After all, if markets are completely efficient, information ceases to have private benefit. Each trader in the market believes he or she will remain just as well informed simply by watching the prices of securities as by undertaking costly and time-consuming research, so there is no reason for any individual to investigate the prospects of a particular investment. But if no one does research, the price system itself will contain less information about the securities being traded, offering potential profits for any individual trader who is able to become better informed. When no one is doing research, the market would operate more efficiently if someone would start, but no individual has the incentive to undertake costly research whose fruits others could enjoy at no expense. A perfectly efficient market would break down, and no one would trade.[7]

Trying to determine how efficient markets actually are quickly leads into a mathematical and statistical morass. There have been hundreds of empirical studies analyzing movements in securities prices with the aid of controversial computer-driven statistical procedures. In general, they point to the same conclusion: financial markets are fairly efficient but far from completely efficient. Price movements do offer smart investors significant opportunities for profit. Although both historical data and new information relating to a stock or a bond are quickly digested by investors, the market often fails to take full account of information known only by a handful of individuals, even when it causes a change in a security's price. Inside information about a company's plans can give a trader an edge for days or even months, and other investors are often slow to guess exactly what their competitors know by observing their actions.[8] Private research has also been found to offer a competitive edge, as some investors do appear to have successful methods of determining which securities are likely to rise or fall in value faster than the market as a whole.[9] Nor does efficient market theory suffice to explain interest rates: the differences in the rates on six-month U.S. Treasury bills and on twenty-year government bonds have varied far more than investors' changing expectations of inflation would warrant.[10]

There are two principal reasons why stock, bond, and commodity exchanges fall short of perfect efficiency. One is the extreme difficulty of evaluating investment risk. By definition, in an efficient market an investment with higher risks should offer higher rewards. But there is no simple, scientific way of determining the risk of an investment, much less of comparing the relative riskiness of several choices. Stock market experts often attempt to quantify risk by looking at a technical measure of volatility, known as "beta," that is supposed to show how volatile a given stock's price is relative to the market as a whole. But betas, which are based on historical performance, have a poor record of predicting which stocks will fluctuate more than the market average.[11] In the bond markets, the well-known bond ratings services, which are paid large fees to evaluate the soundness of bond issues, have often failed to foresee circumstances that would make it harder for an issue to service its bonds, circumstances that became apparent only when a scheduled payment was missed. Although stocks in general are regarded as less risky than, say, commodity futures contracts, there is no way to determine whether the difference in the returns expected from Eaton Corporation common stock and a Chicago Mercantile Exchange contract for delivery of pork bellies next March is enough to make up fully for the difference in risk. And even if an investor guesses the current risks accurately, once a company in which he or she has invested has raised capital it may decide to engage in riskier activities, changing the risk calculus *after* the investor has made a commitment.

All of these factors make it impossible to predict the risks involved in any given investment. Yet without an accurate assessment of risk, an investor can never be sure that a high-risk investment offers a large enough return to make up for the greater odds that the investment will be lost. In that case the market cannot possibly operate efficiently.

The other cause of the market's shortcomings is one that many economists are loath to recognize: human psychology. The efficient markets model postulates an investor with rational expectations, concerned only to maximize profits consistent with the amount of risk he or she is willing to accept. But the people who actually engage in securities transactions, whether for themselves or on behalf of others, seem not to operate on such a ruthlessly rational basis. Matters not directly related to a company's operations or its earnings prospects—fads, fashions, changing social tastes—have much to do with changes in stock prices. When the social mood is optimistic, newcomers flock to play the stock market, driving up prices in the process; when attitudes are pessimistic, they withdraw and prices fall, although there may be no decline in any particular company's inflation-adjusted earnings, dividends, or future prospects.[12] Biotechnology companies' stocks may soar as investors work themselves into a frenzy about the industry's bright future, while the stocks of conglomerates, high flyers in the 1960s, suffer from the craze for corporate specialization in the 1980s. Even hard-bitten money managers for pension funds and insurance companies get swept up in fads. The first scientifically controlled study of the motives of professional money managers found that those who invested in rapidly appreciating stocks with high price-to-earnings ratios "appeared caught up in growth potential, and far less concerned with whether this potential was already reflected in the stock's current market price."[13]

The notion that psychological factors might cause markets to operate at less than full efficiency is anathema to economists who work from the assumption that individuals always act in a completely rational way. To shed light on the issue, a little-known group of experimental economists has studied individuals' behavior in controlled market situations. The experimental findings dispel the notion that a market will settle on a single "correct" price for a security or a commodity, as efficient market theory requires. Instead, the price of a given security may vary widely depending upon how the market is organized.

If traders must publicly post the prices at which they are willing to sell, for example, prices will systematically be higher than in a market without posted prices.[14] The trading rules used on most stock and commodity exchanges, in which the highest current offer to buy and the lowest current offer to sell are both posted but other offers are not, result in relatively efficient markets. On the other hand, many bonds are sold to the highest bidder in sealed-bid auctions, a method that systematically leads to higher bids than do certain types of oral auctions.[15] The financial markets cannot possibly be fully efficient if a security's price depends upon the trading rules.

Under any set of rules, traders learn from experience, and the array of prices paid for a particular security or futures contract will eventually converge toward a single price that accurately reflects supply and demand. In that sense, markets tend to be fairly efficient. That movement toward greater efficiency, however, may be slow. In the meanwhile, changes such as the entry of new participants can disrupt learning and temporarily lead the market astray, making it less efficient. There is no assurance that any market will ever reach full efficiency.[16]

The arcane debate about market efficiency has great importance, not only for borrowers and investors in the financial markets, but for the economy as a whole. For investors, of course, the absence of full efficiency means that playing the markets may be profitable, with money to be made by spotting opportunities for gain or loss that are not yet reflected in market prices. For a company or a government agency issuing stock or bonds, it means that raising money is not just a matter of paying whatever the market demands. The way in which the securities are sold to investors may well affect the prices buyers offer.[17] And for both parties, it means that a would-be acquirer's offer to pay a premium for a company's stock does not mean that the company is badly managed at present or that the acquirer would be able to enhance its value.

Why else would someone pay more for the stock than it's trading for now? Perhaps traders have erroneously attached too low a value to the stock in the past and the acquirer, spotting the market's inefficiency, has located an opportunity to profit. Or perhaps the present management and the acquirer simply have different time frames: management may be pursuing a plan to achieve the greatest possible return for shareholders over a ten-year period by investing cash in research projects that offer no chance of a short-term payout, while the acquirer may want to increase the return as much as possible right now even if that would result in a smaller payback over the long run. An individual investor may come out ahead by taking the immediate profits offered by the acquirer and investing them elsewhere—but then again, it is entirely possible that both the investor and society would have been better off if management had been able to bring its research program to fruition. The question as to which course is economically more efficient comes down to whether the old management that undertook the research program or the new owner that put a stop to it was more correct in assessing the program's likely future returns. That question cannot be answered until the research program is completed, of course, and if the program is discontinued it can never be answered at all.

When markets are inefficient, the commitment of society's savings for friendly acquisitions, hostile tender offers, leveraged buyouts, and the like is not necessarily the most socially productive use of funds. As in the example just given, even if such transactions result in large profits for private individuals, the economy as a whole may not be better off. Under conditions of inefficiency, the fact that such deals are profitable for private investors does not

mean that they increase the wealth of society, and the relative returns of two different investments no longer provide a clue as to
which is socially more valuable. The economy's total output might
well have grown faster if investors' money had been used to build
an oil refinery rather than to fund Allied-Signal's purchase of Bendix
Corporation, or if the $6 billion spent to transform Beatrice Foods
into a private company in 1984 had been used to renovate abandoned houses instead. But in a free market that is not fully efficient,
some socially profitable investments may fail to occur simply because some other investment promises a higher *private* return.

This misallocation of capital due to market inefficiency can
have serious economic consequences. One example is the phenomenon economists call "credit rationing." An individual lender or
investor cannot determine the riskiness of a prospective borrower's
project simply by looking at the market price, because the market
lacks enough information to assess risks accurately. The sensible
investor will demand a risk premium to deal with this uncertainty,
raising the average rate of return insisted upon to cover whatever
unsuspected risks arise. But although that makes sense to the investor, it makes no sense to a borrower with a low-risk project, who
sees that the rate he or she is being charged assumes the project is
riskier than it actually is. Conversely, borrowers whose projects actually entail above-average risks are getting a bargain because they
know there is a good chance the undertakings will fail and no repayment will be made. Low-risk projects, whose owners know the
chance they will actually have to pay the high rates is good, are
priced out of the market, while borrowers have incentives to take
on higher-risk endeavors. That, however, drives up the average
riskiness of the remaining projects, forcing the investor to demand
an even higher risk premium. Eventually, only very highly speculative projects will actually be undertaken, because those are the only
projects that—if they succeed—can generate enough income to
repay the investor. Low-risk, low-return endeavors will not be
funded, because imperfect information keeps the market from correctly identifying them.

Credit rationing of this sort hurts the economy in several ways.
It misallocates investment capital, steering resources into high-risk
speculation and away from more conservative ventures that might

do more to improve society's economic welfare. It faces all firms with higher borrowing costs than they would have in a perfect market, which means that they will borrow less, reducing the total amount of investment in the economy. And the lack of good information about investment risk may actually make business cycles worse, causing investment to fall off more sharply than it otherwise would in a downturn and reducing the effectiveness of government efforts to get the economy moving again.[18]

Clearly, it would be ideal if the government could help make the financial markets efficient. But the imperfections in the financial markets are largely caused by informational problems that the government has no way to resolve. The government is even less likely than private investors to have perfect information about the operations of individual companies and is notoriously overoptimistic when it comes to providing information about the future condition of the economy. It has no way of injecting the truth about risks, corporate plans, or future economic policy into the markets to make them function perfectly.

There are indirect steps the government can take to improve market efficiency. It can require faster and fuller reporting of matters that would affect the price of a security, and it can prohibit insiders from trading on information that has not been made public. It can insist that securities exchanges adopt rules that let prices adjust quickly to changes in supply and demand, and that investors declare the extent and purpose of their securities trading. It can increase investors' own incentives to evaluate the risks of potential investments prudently by minimizing the extent to which government guarantees and insurance programs will cover the cost of investors' mistakes. It can produce and disseminate more economic data. Anything that improves the quality and quantity of the information flowing into the marketplace will help the financial markets function more smoothly.

But once all those steps are taken, the fact remains that the financial markets will fall short of perfect efficiency. As long as that is the case, government officials cannot simply assume that whatever the markets do is best for society. Inefficient markets will not automatically allocate resources in the way that generates the greatest national income or the fastest rate of economic growth. Current market prices and interest rates cannot be assumed to indicate correctly which investments will produce the greatest economic return for society. The fact that individual investors choose to act in a certain way for personal profit does not mean that their actions will be best for the country's welfare.

Correcting this situation may require the government itself to undertake lending and investment on its own. Student loan programs, which are common in industrialized nations, may be the most widespread example of intervention to deal with market inefficiency. Left to its own devices, a bank may be reluctant to make student loans, for which there is typically no collateral that the bank can sell if the student defaults. The probability of repayment depends upon two factors the lender cannot measure. The borrower's willingness to live up to his commitment to repay is hard to determine, because students often have no credit history of their own. The chances that the borrower will use the loan as intended, to train himself to earn enough income to repay what he has borrowed, are also difficult to estimate. These two problems may well lead to market failure: because banks have difficulty distinguishing the good student credit risks from the poor ones, they may make no student loans at all, or may charge such a high rate of interest that honest, studious borrowers do not apply. This market failure can have negative consequences for society by causing too few young people to pursue higher education. A government loan or loan guarantee program may make society better off by increasing the amount of education individuals choose to purchase, even if the government is no better than private bankers at determining the risks involved in lending to individual students.[19]

Unfortunately, there are as yet no neat rules to show when the financial markets are right and when they are wrong. But from what economists have learned to date, there is a valid economic argument for government efforts to slow the pace of corporate takeovers, to regulate the issuance of new types of securities, to prosecute insider trading, and to make sure that credit is available for such uses as housing and student loans. Inefficiencies in the private financial markets may cause the markets not to meet these socially beneficial credit needs. At times, particularly when there is a sudden tightening of monetary policy, those inefficiencies may even lead financial markets to collapse altogether unless the government intervenes to assure the continued availability of credit.

The wisdom of government intervention, of course, needs to be determined from the facts of each specific case. But a government role cannot be rejected automatically in favor of "leaving it to the markets."

7

The Mess in the Currency Markets

O n August 15, 1971, the world took a leap into the unknown. With a stroke of President Richard Nixon's pen, the U.S. government abandoned its century-old pledge to exchange freely dollars for gold. Nixon's move effectively severed the long-standing link between the precious metal and the world's money supply, because foreign governments could no longer use their currencies to buy dollars at a fixed price and then turn those dollars into gold. By December the system in which most major countries with market economies pegged their currencies to the dollar was partially abandoned. Exchange rates were allowed to float.

Like most economic ideas, floating exchange rates were not a recent invention. Several European nations had stopped pegging their currencies in the 1920s, but the results had not been happy. Those flexible arrangements were widely blamed for the decade's volatile exchange rates and huge cross-border capital flows. As a result, when the World War II allies met at Bretton Woods, New Hampshire, in 1944 to plot the shape of the postwar economy, the idea of letting market forces determine currency values was not seriously considered. As Gottfried Haberler, one of the most influential international economists of the time, explained a year later, "It is certain that a system of 'free exchanges' would lead to extremely undesirable results. It would incite capital flight and violent fluctuations. There are very few instances of really free exchanges in monetary history, and none that could be called successful."[1]

The forty-five countries at Bretton Woods agreed that their principal economic goal should be to keep exchange rates stable.

The dollar would serve as the international reserve currency, which the world's central banks would keep on hand to settle their foreign obligations; lest anyone worry about the U.S. government's inclination to print too much money and depreciate its value, the United States pledged that it would convert foreign-owned dollars into gold at any time, at a price of thirty-five dollars an ounce. Each of the other nations then set the international value of its currency in terms of the dollar and agreed to manage its domestic economy so as to keep that exchange rate from fluctuating. In addition, each country was required to contribute both gold and its own currency to the newly created International Monetary Fund. The IMF, in turn, would lend its resources to members needing to bolster their exchange rates. If the French franc were falling sharply against other European currencies, for example, the IMF might lend France gold, British pounds, or German marks. The Bank of France could then use those resources to purchase francs from banks and currency traders, driving their price back up to the agreed-upon level. In return for its loans, the IMF would gain limited oversight of the French economy to make sure that French policies would keep the franc stable in the long run. Countries were permitted to revalue or devalue their currencies if they were fundamentally out of line, but major changes in exchange rates were expected to be the exception rather than the rule.

It was soon evident that the new structure was too rigid. Exchange rates needed to adjust more frequently than the diplomats at Bretton Woods had anticipated, and the system offered no easy way for rates to move. Some economists suggested allowing individual countries to let their exchange rates float occasionally so the markets could determine what the new fixed rate should be,[2] but such cautious proposals were not enough to relieve the increasing stresses on the Bretton Woods system. By the 1960s, basic reform was clearly needed to bring the system in line with major changes in the world economy. The rapid growth of foreign investment and international lending following World War II made it harder for countries to maintain parities that were inconsistent with economic fundamentals, because huge sums of money would flee currencies the markets considered overvalued in search of more economically stable homes.

The problem with fixed exchange rates was simple. It was all well and good to state that the pound sterling was worth $2.80 (U.S.), but in practice that required Britain to make the exchange rate its top economic priority. Should the pound fall, the British government would be forced to raise interest rates, restrict imports, or take some other action to bring the price back to $2.80; if the pound were to rise, the government's policy tools would have to be directed to lowering it. If political pressure to strengthen the domestic economy instead led the government to increase its spending at the risk of inflation, investors would calculate that they could earn better after-inflation returns on their money in other currencies. Buyers would then insist on paying less than the official price for the pound. Without a change in underlying economic conditions, either in Britain or abroad, sterling would remain firm only if central banks joined together to buy huge amounts of the currency to support its price.

This process entailed enormous risks for the central banks: unless they were prepared to commit the unlimited amounts of money needed to assure that everyone with a pound to sell could obtain $2.80 for it, sterling might end up being devalued anyhow—after tons of the currency had piled up in central bank vaults around the world. If that were to occur, of course, the central banks would reap only huge financial losses for their attempts to keep the pound from falling. As speculators became aware that the supply of private capital seeking the highest return was more than enough to overwhelm the central bankers' efforts, currency runs became annual events starting in 1964. Repeatedly, investors dumped sterling and U.S. dollars in favor of deutsche marks and Swiss francs.

To avert such problems and keep their exchange rates in line, more and more nations tried to restrict trade and capital flows to control their citizens' demand for foreign money, a technique that clashed directly with international efforts to eliminate barriers to free trade. With such extreme measures required to maintain it, the fixed rate system was quickly becoming less and less attractive, and the alternative of exchange rate flexibility came to be viewed in a more positive light. In 1966, twenty-seven influential economists published a statement advocating that currencies be allowed to rise or fall several percentage points from their officially pegged rates before countries would be required to change their economic policies. This limited floating would not eliminate adjustment problems, but it did offer the potential for averting a major international financial crisis every time the lira fell 2 percent against the mark. Many of the economists backing the proposal, however, viewed limited floating as a temporary expedient for what they believed to be a brief and abnormal period of heavy speculation in the currency markets, after which the world could move back to fixed rates. Unlimited exchange rate flexibility was still considered far too risky for serious consideration.[3]

Nixon's move to take the United States off the gold standard in 1971 removed the linchpin from the system. While most countries still set official values for their currencies in terms of dollars, these were no longer fixed in terms of some underlying unit of value, such as gold. And though exchange rates were nominally fixed, individual countries were forced to revalue or devalue with increasing frequency. Over the next four years, the IMF sought to patch things back together, temporarily allowing currencies to fluctuate within a limited range, while countries attempted to devise a permanent way of pegging rates that would avoid the problems of the past. But the task was impossible. Going to any variety of fixed-rate system invited more of the turmoil that had caused the Bretton Woods agreement to collapse in the first place. Limited floating, a compromise proposal, wasn't much better: even if currencies were allowed to move freely within a range of 3 percent or 4 percent, exchange rate crises would be inevitable unless the limits were in line with economic fundamentals. Finally, at an IMF meeting in Jamaica in January 1976, attempts to arrange the world's money neatly were abandoned. Exchange rates were allowed to float freely.

The switch to "clean floating" represented a major victory for believers in free and unfettered markets. Complete deregulation of foreign exchange markets had been an extreme idea back when Milton Friedman first proposed it in 1950,[4] but its purported advantages and the evident disadvantages of other approaches changed many minds. Gottfried Haberler, for example, conquered his fear that flexibility would make exchange rates extremely volatile; instead, he acknowledged, floating rates could go hand in hand with economic stability, so long as countries pursued sound monetary and fiscal policies.[5]

Flexible rates were said to offer important economic benefits. First, and most important, they would allow individual countries to pursue divergent economic policies. Under fixed rates, if Britain chose fast money supply growth to stimulate its economy while Germany pursued tight money, the policy difference would automatically lead to an international exchange rate crisis. Either Britain would have to devalue the pound or Germany would have to revalue the mark. With rates free to vary, however, each country could act according to its own priorities to fight inflation, ease unemployment, or smooth the path of domestic growth. Exchange rates would simply vary in the process, moving a little bit each day, and the feelings of national shame attached to a deliberate devaluation would be banished.

Flexible rates also promised a painless way of resolving trade imbalances. If Italy imports more than it exports, it needs dollars, marks, and yen to pay for those surplus imports. Under the fixed-rate system, unless Italian investments abroad earned enough to make up the difference, the country had only two choices. It could borrow abroad, or it could use the foreign currency reserves of its central bank to pay off those obligations. In the face of a trade deficit that persisted for several years, however, the central bank would eventually run out of foreign exchange, and strict import controls would be needed to bring imports into line with exports. Flexible rates, by contrast, are theoretically self-correcting. When Italians lined up to buy foreign currency to pay for their excess imports, their eagerness to sell lire would drive down its price relative to foreign currencies, making imported goods dearer in Italy and Italian exports cheaper abroad. The trade deficit would automatically be evened out.[6]

The third major benefit claimed by supporters of the new regime was smoother economic adjustment. Changes in the fixed rate system usually occurred only when one country's currency had gotten very far out of line. As a result, when changes did occur, they tended to be large; after resisting devaluation for years, Britain was forced to lower the pound's dollar value suddenly by a hefty 17 percent in November 1967. Such massive changes over short time periods caused major economic dislocations and disrupted business planning. With floating rates, on the other hand, economists anticipated that currency values would change gradually, on a daily basis, as individuals updated their expectations of each country's economic policies. These smaller, more frequent exchange rate movements would allow importers, exporters, and investors to adjust to economic change in a much more orderly fashion.

Finally, flexible exchange rates were supposed to result in increased economic efficiency for the world as a whole. If a country's currency were overvalued in a fixed-rate system, foreign goods would be artificially cheap compared with domestic merchandise. The price of, say, imported television sets would be unrealistically low compared with the price of domestically made radios, leading consumers to buy too many of the former and too few of the latter in complete disregard of the overall economic costs of making the different products. Under floating rates and free trade, by contrast, the relative prices of goods that are traded internationally should always be the same from country to country, so individual buying decisions would accurately reflect relative costs—the precondition economic theory sets for maximum economic efficiency. The same conditions of efficiency were expected to be true for capital: market forces would assure that the total expected return on an investor's money, considering risks, expected interest payments, and likely exchange rate changes, would be the same in every country. If the total return on an investment appeared higher in any one currency than in another, investors would flock to that currency, driving up its price and eliminating the differential. That market action would make for the most efficient possible allocation of capital among countries. By helping consumers and investors in all countries to make decisions that would result in a more efficient use of resources, flexible rates were expected to achieve a higher level of economic output for the entire world.

The case for freeing the exchange markets was not ironclad, of course. Instability, leading to turmoil in the currency markets and to unforeseen shifts in exchange rates, was a major concern. Proponents of flexible rates acknowledged that possibility, but they judged it a plus rather than a minus because the risk of massive exchange rate changes would force governments to pursue responsible economic policies. As Milton Friedman contended, "If floating rates are highly unstable, it will be because the internal monetary policies of the countries or some other aspects of their economy are highly unstable."[7]

Through its first few years, the floating rate system seemed to confirm the hopes of its proponents. In general, rates changed slowly and gradually. Although some currencies were very volatile—the German mark, worth 29.5 U.S. cents in August 1971, bought 43 cents in July 1973, fell to 36 cents six months later, and bounced back to 44 cents by early 1975—exchange rate movements were actually fairly smooth when each currency was measured against a basket of others, rather than simply against one other currency. The new system did not disrupt world trade, as skeptics had feared, in part because the fast-developing currency futures markets enabled importers and exporters to hedge their risks. Trade patterns were found to adjust to exchange rate changes more slowly than many economists had expected, but sooner or later a falling currency would improve a country's balance of trade. All in all, the unrestrained international currency market appeared to work smoothly.[8]

That optimism was rudely shattered in the decade starting in 1978. As U.S. inflation soared toward double-digit levels, the stability of flexible exchange rates collapsed. The dollar fell 13.8 percent against a basket of major currencies between September 1977 and September 1978. After flattening out through 1980, it reversed direction. Even as the Federal Reserve Board was driving interest rates to record highs to purge the economy of inflation, the Reagan administration's economic program dramatically cut government revenues without cutting spending. The combination of tight money and loose fiscal policy forced the government to borrow unprecedented sums at sky-high interest rates. Foreigners wanted to get in on the high interest rates too, and their demand for dollars propelled the currency higher and higher, nearly doubling its value (as measured against other currencies weighted according to their importance in international trade) between September 1980 and February 1985.

Then, as suddenly as it had begun, the buying frenzy stopped. By February 1987 the dollar had collapsed almost back to the level of 1980. Then, after the finance ministers of major free market economies announced that it had reached the correct level, central banks intervened on an unprecedented scale to stabilize the dollar. Although the total amount of dollars purchased by the major central banks has never been revealed, experts estimate that they spent the equivalent of $80 billion in German marks and Japanese yen during 1987 and early 1988 in order to prop up the dollar's price. And the dollar was not the only currency on a roller coaster. The value of the British pound, measured against the currencies of seventeen other industrial countries, rose 13.8 percent during a six-month period in early 1986, then fell 12.4 percent over the subsequent year. Japan's yen unexpectedly climbed 39 percent between August 1985 and August 1986. The Dutch guilder gained over 17 percent during an eighteen-month period in 1985 and 1986, while the German mark was rising more than 16 percent.

These exchange rate movements are not adequately explained simply by labeling them as expressions of investors' rational expectations of future economic changes. Indeed, there is evidence that rates prevailing in world currency markets have been dramatically out of line with forecasts of economic conditions. The differences in U.S. and foreign interest rates and inflation rates, for example, were not nearly high enough in the period from 1982 to 1986 to account for the extent of the dollar's rise. While high real interest rates provided the impetus for foreigners to flock to the dollar in 1982, the spreads between real interest rates in New York and those in Frankfurt or Tokyo were never so great as to justify a near doubling of the dollar's price in marks or yen. Even more puzzling, the dollar continued to skyrocket in 1984, even though falling U.S. interest rates should have been driving it down and economic forecasters were widely predicting its imminent decline.[9]

Rather than basing their choices of which nations' currencies to hold on a cold-blooded calculation of which investments will generate the highest after-inflation return, it appears that speculators often surrender to the temptation to bet on a trend. A rapidly rising dollar will pull in speculators betting on the dollar's further rise, in defiance of all economic fundamentals, and their purchases will of course drive the currency to yet higher levels. As long as the public believes the dollar will keep rising and backs that belief with its money, the dollar will continue to climb, following the classic pattern of speculative bubbles. Once something happens to puncture the bubble, however, the currency will depreciate quickly despite the lack of hard economic data to justify such a gloomy view. Just as such seemingly irrational behavior is at work in the securities markets, foreign exchange markets appear to be heavily influenced by psychological factors: a conviction that economic fundamentals are not captured by the latest statistics, a desire not to miss out on easy profits from a rising currency, a readiness to join the crowd in selling rather than being caught with stocks of a falling currency that other traders have dumped. These factors keep the foreign exchange markets operating inefficiently, despite the best efforts of every individual market participant to keep well informed about current conditions in currency markets around the world.[10] If the markets are inefficient, of course, insightful speculators have the opportunity to reap profits systematically from currency trading. But more importantly for the global economy, the market-determined prices of freely floating exchange rates will not necessarily be the "right" prices, the prices that will maximize the world's economic welfare.

According to the theories of free market economics, the world's economies should have been able to adjust to the exchange rate gyrations of the 1980s costlessly and efficiently. But in a world in which businesses and individuals must make long-term commitments without being able to hedge their risks perfectly, adapting to changed exchange rates proved anything but costless. Starting in 1982, factories in the United States suddenly found their products unable to compete in world markets for no reason other than the fact that the currency with which they paid workers and purchased equipment had dramatically increased in value against the currencies in which their foreign competitors did business. U.S. exports collapsed while imports soared, driving the economy from a small $28 billion merchandise trade deficit in 1981 to an enormous $153 billion dollar trade gap in 1987. Flexible exchange rates did not automatically correct this imbalance, as they were supposed to. Instead, the U.S. government's massive borrowing needs kept U.S. interest rates high, pushing the dollar ever higher despite trade deficits of unprecedented size.

Though the dollar reached its peak in February 1985, it took two more years before the U.S. trade deficit began to diminish, and even then improvement was slow. Foreigners, it turns out, tend to price their goods according to the price structure in their export markets rather than according to their costs back home, so import prices tend to be even stickier than the prices of domestic goods; import prices in the United States rose far more gradually than the dollar fell. In addition, industries in which American producers had been leaders, from electronics to commuter airplanes to machine tools, were now dominated by foreign competitors who had used five years of highly favorable exchange rates to get through the high-cost stage of learning to make new products. By the time the dollar began to decline, these foreign companies had managed to learn enough to be competitive even without a currency advantage. The falling dollar may eventually bring U.S. trade into balance, but it will not restore individual companies or industries to the positions they had in world markets before the exchange rate rose.[11]

On the trade front, then, the flexible exchange rate system hasn't quite lived up to its advance billing. The effects of an over-valued currency are not always easily reversible when the exchange rate changes. Nor do trade deficits disappear as quickly and easily as advocates of flexible rates had imagined.

Economic adjustment was also far less smooth and gradual than had been expected with a floating rate system. While the U.S. dollar was high, hundreds of thousands of manufacturing workers lost their jobs as companies shifted production offshore or rushed to automate their remaining factories at home in an effort to avoid high labor costs. The costs of this tumultuous shake-up, in terms both of the unused skills and training of laid-off workers and of prematurely abandoned plants and production machinery, cannot be quantified, but they were undoubtedly enormous: in the United States, employment in manufacturing and mining fell 4.5 percent from 1980 to August 1985 largely because of the overvalued dollar. And the costs were not borne by the United States alone. After the strong dollar began its collapse in 1985, Japanese manufacturers, who had constructed massive capacity to make goods for export during a period when 1 dollar would buy 250 yen, suddenly found their factories uncompetitive at 150 yen to the dollar. They too were forced to close down suddenly unprofitable plants, to lay off workers, and to transfer production to countries with more favorable exchange rates, including the United States. Instead of smoothing the process of adjustment to changing economic conditions, flexible exchange rates led to faster and larger shifts of production and employment from one country to another than had ever been required in the days of fixed rates.

Far from increasing economic efficiency, the floating rate regime has resulted in a major drain on the world's growth. Perfectly good factories must be abandoned far before the end of their useful lives while new facilities to make the same products are erected on other continents, solely because the change in currency values makes production in one country or another uncompetitive. In some industries, multinational firms now deliberately build excess capacity dispersed throughout the world so they can always obtain a supply of their products from the lowest-cost country—a strategic approach to dealing with volatile exchange rates which is perfectly rational from the viewpoint of an individual firm but wasteful for the world economy. And each time one plant closes and another opens elsewhere, skilled workers are left unemployed, rendering worthless massive investments in training and education.

This constant and unpredictable movement of manufacturing is a far cry from traditional free market explanations of how "comparative advantage" determines which countries produce which types of products. In a world with cleanly floating currency, considerations such as output per worker, access to labor supplies, and proximity to natural resources are less important than whether a country's exchange rate is high or low. That fact has made each nation's money into a strategic tool in international economic competition. Every country has strong reason to keep its currency undervalued in an effort to make its products competitive in foreign countries and to make imports expensive at home, maintaining low unemployment without resorting to tariffs, quotas, and other overt methods of protecting domestic industries. Thus the fact that an industry has established itself in a given country can no longer be taken as a sign that that location is the spot on the globe in which the product can be manufactured most efficiently; instead, it may signify only that the country's exchange rate is attractive to exporters.

Floating rates have also harmed economic efficiency by contributing to the distortion of relative prices in many economies. In a world with free trade and flexible currencies, if Britain's currency rises sharply against France's, British prices for cars, television sets, and other items sensitive to foreign competition will fall compared with prices for haircuts, newspapers, and restaurant meals. In France, conversely, the less valuable franc means that prices of imports, and of domestically made goods that compete with imports, will increase relative to prices of nontraded goods.

So long as the new exchange rate is an accurate reflection of underlying economic factors, that's all to the good. In that case, exchange rates will shift permanently, changing each country's prices in such a way as to encourage more efficient use of resources on both sides. But if the new rates do not correctly indicate long-term changes in the two countries' economies—if, for example, they are driven up above a reasonable long-term level by feverish speculation, by incorrect expectations of the actions of the two governments, or by a systematic tendency of currencies to "overshoot" the correct exchange rate and rise or fall further than they should—then the resulting price changes will lead to a misallocation of resources. Britons will buy more traded goods and fewer nontraded ones than they would if the pound were at its "correct" long-run level against the franc, while Frenchmen will be overspending on nontradeables and underspending on traded consumer goods. The low relative price of haircuts in Paris will lead strong demand, inducing too many Frenchmen to open barber shops, many of which will fail when the relative price of traded goods falls to a more normal level and the relative price of haircuts rises. Whether a given shift in exchange rates makes an economy more or less efficient is difficult to know at the time, but the temporary nature of many changes in currency prices suggests that inefficiency, not higher output, is often the result.[12]

The other promised benefit of floating exchange rates was that they would allow each country to pursue independently its own economic policies. This advantage too has proved illusory. If anything, maintaining a system of flexible exchange rates requires far more consultation among countries than the fixed-rate system ever did. Such matters as the large U.S. budget deficit, restrictive German money supply growth, and Japan's policies to encourage individual savings and discourage consumption have repeatedly been the subjects of contentious international wrangling. With exchange rates free to vary, any "domestic" economic policy that affects inflation, interest rates, or the demand for goods and services will have direct international repercussions in the currency markets, on trade flows, and on patterns of cross-border investment. But the unpredictability of those repercussions has made it far harder for governments and central banks to set economic policy under the floating rate regime than it was in the days of fixed rates.

This instability is directly contrary to the expectations attending the abandonment of fixed exchange rates. Proponents of floating rates assumed that noninflationary monetary policies on all sides would be enough to keep the system stable. The basic concept was that governments should reserve their monetary tools to keep the exchange rate at the appropriate level, while using fiscal policies, such as spending and taxing authority, if they wanted to pump their economy up or slow it down. But even the most conservative, non-inflationary monetary policies haven't been enough to avoid large exchange rate fluctuations. Money supply management alone cannot do the job; differences among countries in interest rates, government spending plans, and tax policies can also make the currency markets quake, even if every central bank follows a non-inflationary path. Nor is some outrageous government action required to set the exchange markets on edge. Currencies may bounce unpredictably in the markets although each individual government appears to be pursuing reasonable economic policies.[13]

Moreover, the tightly interwoven world economy means that all nations, including those with sound economic management, may see their exchange rates destabilized by the actions of others. The large U.S. budget deficits since 1982 have dramatically affected the value of the Swiss franc against the Mexican peso just as surely as they have changed the dollar's price in terms of yen. Because of the United States' importance to the economies of both countries, particularly Mexico, such fluctuations were inevitable even if both countries had maintained stringent noninflationary policies.

These complex global interconnections caused by floating rates have hampered the efforts of individual countries to employ their traditional monetary and fiscal policy tools to achieve specific goals, such as driving unemployment below 4 percent or keeping the prime interest rate at the 6 percent level. To begin with, economists have only the poorest understanding of how exchange rates will respond to a change in government policy. They are even less able to predict the next step—how much the new exchange rates will increase or decrease the flow of privately owned capital into the country. The inability to forecast these changes makes it difficult to estimate whether any given government policy move will reverberate largely within the domestic economy or whether it will be felt most strongly abroad.

With fixed exchange rates, expansionary fiscal policies such as large government budget deficits quickly pump up the domestic economy, at least temporarily, both by making more money available for consumption and by encouraging businesses to invest. With flexible rates, however, a large budget deficit also drives the exchange rate up, making imports cheap and exports dear, which reduces the domestic economic gains. Conversely, although lower government spending has traditionally been labeled "contractionary," cutting budgets in an open economy need not slow the economy. In the United States, for example, economists disagree strongly about the net effect of sharply reducing the federal budget deficit. Clearly, a lower deficit will reduce domestic spending, but by reducing government borrowing needs it will also drive the dollar down, potentially cutting imports and increasing exports enough actually to increase total economic output. Furthermore, talk of "cutting the deficit" misses an important point: the effects of budget cutbacks will differ greatly depending on exactly what cuts are made. One dollar less spent on goods and services that are not traded internationally, such as government office staff, will slow the economy far more than a dollar cut from government purchases of steel, computers, or other internationally traded goods.[14]

Monetary policy has also lost some of its predictability, for similar reasons. Suppose, for example, that Germany's Bundesbank faces heavy pressure to lower German interest rates and stimulate the country's economy. In the days of the Bretton Woods system, Bundesbank directors could guess with reasonable accuracy how much and how quickly a 1 percent reduction of the interest rate on their loans to commercial banks would affect the German economy. Today, however, with flexible rates and few restrictions on the flow of capital from one country to another, the Bundesbank's move will cause the mark to fall at the same time as it drives German interest rates lower. Investors will respond by shifting their money out of marks and into other currencies in which they can earn higher inflation-adjusted interest. That flight from the mark will limit the fall of interest rates, and that will in turn make the Bundesbank's effort less effective in stimulating economic growth. Exactly how far the Bundesbank needs to lower interest rates to achieve the stimulus it wants is impossible to estimate in advance, because the net effect on Germany's economy depends critically upon how much capital moves abroad.[15]

On all these counts, then, flexible exchange rates have not fulfilled their promise to stabilize the world economy automatically. They may even have made things worse, by offering each individual government within the floating rate system the opportunity to pursue its own economic goals at the expense of other countries. With floating rates, there is virtue in weakness: a relatively undervalued currency helps exports and curbs imports, creating jobs in sectors where foreign-made goods would otherwise hold sway. This poses a temptation for every country facing an unemployment problem. By keeping its currency from rising against those of its trading partners, it can force other countries to run trade deficits or to bear the costs of changes in the world economy. This type of international game playing by governments and central banks was not possible when exchange rates were fixed. Officially, of course, government management of exchange rates is against the rules by which a completely unregulated exchange rate system must live. But since almost everything a government does affects its exchange rates, who is to draw the line and claim that the current monetary policy of the Bank of France is designed to keep the franc low rather than to meet some legitimate domestic economic goal? The temptation to cheat on the system is enormous. Once governments begin to do so, many of the benefits a floating rate system offers may quickly disappear.

The evidence of the past decade suggests that free markets in currencies don't work as well in practice as they do in the equations and diagrams of economic theorists. But the all-too-evident shortcomings of laissez-faire alone are not enough to justify an interventionist approach to managing exchange rates. Any proposal to get the world's governments back in the business of controlling the price of currencies must show not only that floating rates are imperfect, but that activist government policies will work better.

A return to Bretton Woods is out of the question: there is no reason to imagine that fixed exchange rates will work any more smoothly in the 1990s than they did in the 1960s, and the United States, which incurred substantial costs by making its currency the linchpin of the international monetary system for the quarter-century following World War II, seems unlikely to volunteer for that role again. Although there have been occasional calls for a return to fixing the value of each currency in terms of an ounce of gold, a specific quantity of other commodities, or in a way that keeps the buying power of wages in different industrialized countries the same,[16] those approaches too offer only the dimmest prospect of improving the situation. Keeping currencies stable against gold or other commodities could result in dramatic inflation or deflation within individual countries as the world's supply of precious metal, grain, or oil changes—hardly a desirable trade-off for exchange rate stability. And, of course, just as in the days of the old gold standard, nations would be unable to target their economic policies to any end save exchange rate stability.

The massive problems involved in any return to fixed rates have led economists to focus on revamping the floating rate system instead, finding ways to allow exchange rates to vary in a limited way without causing chaos in the world economy. If such a system can be established, the world could still reap the benefits floating rates have to offer, both in helping to allocate capital among different countries and in setting the relative prices between traded and non-traded goods within each country. Although flexible rates may not fill those roles perfectly, they are still better able to do so than are exchange rates established in advance by some international agreement. At the same time, most of the approaches now under discussion would put limits on how widely rates would be permitted to fluctuate in an effort to avoid the massive problems that occur when currency speculation drives one currency or another in extreme directions not justified by underlying economic conditions.

One much-debated method, establishing "target zones" within which each currency would be allowed to move against others, is based squarely in the tradition of Bretton Woods. At the start, the governments of participating countries would have to determine the set of exchange rates on which the system would be based. Around each currency's "central rate" against every other currency there would be a target zone within which it could move freely; the mark might be allowed to rise or fall up to 10 percent against the dollar, for example, while the lira might have a target zone 15 percent wide against the pound. Each country in the system would promise to keep its currency within the agreed-upon range; a country that saw its exchange rate fall toward the bottom of the zone would be expected to use tighter monetary policy to keep the rate within the allowable limits. Fairly wide zones, however, would give each government great discretion about the timing of its policy changes, rather than the instant response required with fixed rates.[17]

Within Western Europe, a variant of the target zone approach, the European Monetary System, has achieved modest success in reducing exchange rate instability without leading to higher inflation since its establishment in 1979. But the European economies are much more tightly interlinked with each other than with the economies of the United States, Canada, and Japan, and (except for Britain, which has remained aloof from the EMS) they have implicitly acknowledged the role of Germany's central bank, the Bundesbank, in setting the monetary policies for other nations to follow. Such a willingness to follow a single leader in order to keep exchange rates stable is not evident worldwide, so the EMS may not offer a suitable model for resolving exchange rate problems outside Europe.

In 1987, major countries with market economies opted for a less ambitious approach that does not take aim at exchange rates directly. Instead, economic officials will jointly look at a set of seven specified economic indicators, such as exchange rates, inflation rates, and money growth rates, to evaluate each country's performance. If they believe one country's exchange rate is fundamentally out of line, the countries are supposed to agree jointly on actions to reestablish the proper relationships among their currencies. Exactly what actions can be taken in any given case, however, remains unclear. Despite the readiness of the world's leaders to offer each other economic advice, it is not at all obvious which economic policies each government should pursue even if all agree that the dollar is far too high. And most studies of the effects of international coordination of economic policies indicate that the gains from such measures will be small.[18]

There is no ready answer to the question of which system is better, or whether either is always superior to simply letting rates float without restrictions. As Britain's *Economist* has noted,

"Changing the exchange-rate system, by itself, merely shifts the realm of economic turbulence, it does not abolish it."[19] The choice of how to organize the currency markets depends on what types of economic disturbances and crises are most likely. No single approach is sure to bring about the greatest economic welfare for the world under all types of economic conditions. There is no easy answer.[20]

What is certain is that, in a world in which governments must make economic policy decisions that impinge on exchange rates on a daily basis, the idea that there can truly be "nonintervention" in the currency markets is implausible. Keeping the world's economy healthy will repeatedly require the active involvement of governments to assure that exchange rates do not stray too far from values justified by the prospects for inflation, interest rates, and economic growth in each country.

8
The New Trade Theory

For over a century and a half, every student of elementary economics has learned a basic truth: free trade between nations makes all countries better off. But as economists have looked more closely at the benefits of trade, that simple lesson turns out not to be true. At long last, economists agree that there may be a case for protectionism—at least in theory. If a nation's government guesses right, it might be able to promote certain exports and restrict certain imports so that its own citizens are better off, at the expense of the rest of the world. Such policies are attractive, but they carry a heavy risk: if the government guesses wrong about which products it should favor, or if politics forces choices based on considerations other than economic efficiency, protection will reduce the nation's economic welfare far more than previously believed. In short, while there's now a theoretical rationale for those who oppose allowing a free flow of imports, there are still no easy clues about when protection should be used in practice.

The argument for unrestricted international trade was first stated as long ago as 1821 by the English economist David Ricardo. Ricardo observed that even if one country's production of every conceivable product is more efficient than another country's, trade between the two still makes economic sense. Both nations will be better off if each exports those products it makes most efficiently and then imports the things in which its producers are comparatively inefficient. In general, classical trade theory contends, what an economy produces should reflect its natural endowments. A country with a surplus of workers will have the edge in making labor-intensive products such as shoes and clothing, while a country that can draw on large amounts of savings will focus on capital-intensive industries such as automobiles and electrical products. If both countries act this way, the world's resources will be turned into a larger supply of goods than if the countries each try to be self-sufficient in everything, and citizens of both countries will be able to increase their consumption.

This idea, known as the theory of comparative advantage, inevitably leads to the conclusion that government involvement with trade matters is a bad idea. After all, restrictions on imports cause local citizens to devote resources wastefully to making something they could obtain with less effort simply by importing it. An export subsidy has the same result, since people will spend their time turning out the subsidized product when they could actually create more wealth by doing something else. Of course many individuals may find their personal economic condition much improved if the government interferes with trade, but the country as a whole will suffer.

In this "classical" analysis of trade, since exports and imports make all countries wealthier, measures that interfere with trade must hurt all sides. When the U.S. government puts quotas or tariffs on imports of foreign steel, that harms not only the foreign steel makers but also all American users of steel, who must now pay higher prices. Although some Americans may benefit, such as steel industry workers and the stockholders of steel companies, it is easy to demonstrate that the overall loss to the U.S. economy far outweighs the benefits. One careful study of the textile and apparel industries, for example, estimated that the import quotas and tariffs in force in the United States in 1984 reduced the nation's total output by $6.65 billion, with most of that loss due to the measures' effect in encouraging too much production in the United States; while the restraints "saved" the jobs of an estimated 640,000 workers, they did so at a yearly cost of some $42,000 per job, several times the workers' average annual wages.[1] If markets work freely as classical economics believes, the only time restricting trade actually increases a country's wealth is when the country is such a large player in the world market for a given product that its sales or purchases can change the world price. If, for example, the U.S. government were to restrict exports of soybeans, it is conceivable that foreign demand would drive world soybean prices so high that

American farmers' income would rise rather than fall, at least in the short run, although the long-run effect would be to encourage other countries to grow soybeans.

This simple analysis has been enormously important in influencing the worldwide movement toward freer trade since the 1930s, and its basic correctness has been confirmed in the years since World War II. Repeated agreements among the world's major trading nations to reduce tariffs and eliminate other barriers to international trade have been accompanied by rapid growth in the volume of trade and a steady increase in living standards throughout the industrialized world. Although this increased trade has frequently caused temporary dislocations as workers made redundant by imports are forced to learn new skills, its overall effects have been much as David Ricardo predicted. Consumers have benefited from low prices for manufactures and from the wide diffusion of new products. Industries have been forced to become more efficient to compete internationally. In economists' parlance, the gains from trade have been large.

The events of the 1970s and 1980s, however, have challenged the argument that free trade is best no matter what the circumstances. Among the most striking international developments of these decades is the rapid transformation of Japan. Until the 1970s Japan was known principally for its cheap imitations of foreign products. But in an astonishingly brief period, the country became a leading manufacturer of sophisticated machinery, electronic equipment, and consumer goods. This overnight change flies in the face of what traditional trade theory would predict: Japan maintains both legal and social barriers that keep foreign goods out, and economists normally assume that such barriers will lead to inefficient domestic industries with little innovative spirit. In the Japanese case, however, many experts argue that the government's protectionist policies have made it profitable for manufacturers to enter fields that otherwise would have been dominated by foreign companies, enabling the country to increase its wealth at a far faster rate than if there had been no interference with free trade.

During the same period, nations such as Taiwan, Korea, and Brazil have moved from being "underdeveloped countries" to the status of newly industrializing nations with large manufacturing sectors capable of producing a wide array of goods. This was not simply the result of an eager private sector at work; rather, the governments of those countries carefully selected which industries they wanted to promote, protected them against import competition, and restricted domestic competitors as well to provide guaranteed profits for the chosen firms. These government efforts to promote new industries have clearly accelerated the pace of economic development in certain countries, despite a vast academic literature insisting that protection of "infant industries" is inefficient and unproductive. The old theories seem not to apply to the world of the late twentieth century.

Reshaping economic theory to take this new evidence of the potential benefits of government intervention into account has preoccupied international economists for the past decade. Their new research has in no way overturned the basic arguments for free trade. But it has also revealed an enormously complex case for departing from free trade, a case that has transformed the way every economist looks at the question of who wins and who loses when trade occurs.

Like all of classical economics, traditional trade theory is built on the critical assumption of market clearing. This means, of course, that there is perfect competition among both buyers and sellers, so that no one company or country can influence the world price by itself. There cannot be massive economies of scale, for if there were, the first country to establish large-scale production would always be able to underprice everyone else and keep them out of the market. Perfect competition assumes too that labor and capital are perfectly flexible, so that workers and equipment can shift costlessly from making one good to producing something else. It requires that there be no barriers to entry, such as the need to sink large amounts of unrecoverable funds into a research program or a huge distribution network before entering a new field. Finally, every person is assumed to be able to hedge completely the risks of involvement in the international economy by purchasing insurance, commodity futures contracts, and currency futures in whatever quantity he or she desires.

In practice, of course, perfect competition is nowhere to be found. As long as competition functions well, the lack of perfection is not always critical. But increasingly, it seems, world trade does not work in the way Ricardo foresaw. Where the theory of comparative advantage suggests that trade will occur between countries with very different endowments of labor, capital, and natural resources, in fact most trade takes place among countries with relatively similar economies. The United States is the major importer of cars from Canada—but is also the main exporter of cars *to* Canada. Germany ships its steel across the border to Belgium but buys Belgian steel in return. But if Germany has a comparative advantage over Belgium that allows it to export steel, Belgium cannot simultaneously have the same comparative advantage over Germany! Something else must be at work.

That something is what economists call "monopolistic competition," competition among firms that each have a monopoly in a specific product but whose product is similar enough to other firms' products that buyers may switch from one to the other. While there are some goods—corn, perhaps, or cocoa, or raw copper—that are pretty much the same everywhere, producers of most types of products work hard to distinguish them from similar goods produced by others. Sometimes, differentiation depends more on marketing or packaging than on the characteristics of the product itself. In other instances, producers use proprietary techniques, such as a special combination of materials or a patented technological process, to make their good different from others. These differentiated products account for much of world trade. Although Germany and Belgium sell each other steel, each country is likely to specialize in certain types of steel products rather than producing every possible item. This approach lowers costs by allowing manufacturers to build their plants at whatever size allows for most efficient production, rather than building small factories everywhere so that each country is self-sufficient in everything.

Instead of competing with an existing German steel company by making the exact same girder, the Belgian producer may well decide to turn out a slightly thinner or wider steel girder that can also be sold internationally. By aiming at the international market, both companies can build factories of a size that offers the lowest cost per girder, rather than having the factory's size dictated by the demand for girders in any one country. For most industrialized countries, specialized production of this sort has been the key to achieving a high level of income. Belgium may be too small to consume everything its steel mills would make if they turned out a complete line of steel products in enough quantity to operate efficiently. If the mills operate at lower capacity just to meet the country's needs, on the other hand, the cost per ton of steel will be high. By producing some items for both the domestic and foreign markets and importing other types of steel, Belgium's industry can operate efficiently. Which types will Belgium make? There is no way to predict the answer. Historical accident, such as the presence of a university research lab or the chance establishment of a particular industry in one location at some time in the past, is as important as economics in determining the pattern of production. Since Belgium and its major trading partners are likely to have similar economies, no comparative advantage is involved.[2]

Monopolistic competition offers an important advantage for producers: to a certain degree, they can control their own destinies. In the highly competitive world wheat market, market forces will keep prices low enough that individual farmers can earn only a modest return on their investments, and nothing the farmer himself can do will enable him to receive a higher price. In a monopolistically competitive industry, on the other hand, a producer can often boost profits by raising prices higher than they would be under perfect competition, since no one else sells precisely the same good. The producer can't raise prices too high, of course, because customers will switch to the similar but slightly different good produced by someone else. In addition, the juicy profits will attract direct competitors, and the price premium will fall. For the producer, then, monopolistic competition isn't as good as full-scale monopoly, but it is far more profitable than head-to-head competition.

In the domestic economy, we usually look upon these "monopoly rents" with disfavor, because they represent extra money taken from the pockets of consumers. In the international economy, on the other hand, part of monopoly rents comes out of the hides of the foreigners who have imported a given item. The extra price those foreigners pay comes back to the exporting country in the form of higher wages for the workers and higher dividends for the shareholders of the monopoly enterprise. The exporter's national economy is better off.

Viewing international trade in a framework of monopolistic competition has important consequences for trade policy. If a government is able to intervene correctly, it can help companies based in its country to export and obtain monopoly rents—excess profits—from foreigners, while doing its best to keep foreign companies from extracting similar monopoly rents from its own citizens. Conversely, if the government fails to intervene, the foreigners may be able to commandeer part of its country's wealth through their high prices. Government can no longer watch from the sidelines. So long as monopolies or oligopolies exist, the extra profits are there for the taking, and if one country doesn't get them another will.

Instead of being a means to improve the welfare of all sides, trade policy under monopolistic competition becomes a strategic tool by which to get the better of one's neighbors. As two trade scholars, Gene M. Grossman and J. David Richardson, noted in 1985, "In some cases, if participants are competing for shares of a pie of roughly fixed size, trade policy is bound to be contentious. In other cases, strategic behavior may dictate cooperation that can lead to mutual benefit. In all cases, however, the standard tenets of the orthodox theory of trade policy may fail to apply."[3]

Take the simple case of a product made by only two companies in the entire world. One of the producers, an American firm, competes with a single foreign company in some third country abroad. Because the lack of perfect competition means prices are above the market-clearing level, the American firm makes a heady profit on each sale, a profit that flows back to workers and shareholders at home and thus makes the United States better off. The foreign competitor does the same. The United States is prospering at the expense of citizens of the third country, who are paying high prices for their goods, but it could garner even more money if the American company could grab some of the foreign firm's profits. If the U.S. government steps in to subsidize the American firm's exports, it will be able to underprice the foreign company, expand its market share, and, in essence, steal some of its monopoly rents.

Of course, the American company could try to lower prices and increase market share on its own, without government help, but the foreigners would counter with a similar move in hopes of outlasting it. They might even seek a subsidy from their government to help them undercut the Americans. If the U.S. government is involved from the beginning, however, and backs the American company in making the first move, the American company's demand for a larger slice of the pie will be far more credible, and the foreigners might decide not to fight. With a properly calculated export subsidy and no foreign retaliation, the American company will gain far more in foreign profits than the U.S. government is paying out in subsidies, and the economy of the United States will become wealthier as a result.

When the foreign government responds by subsidizing its company's exports as the U.S. government has, on the other hand, things look different. Both companies will produce too much, driving down prices around the world and cutting profits on both sides. The subsidies then become unproductive, and both countries will gain from a joint agreement to eliminate them and revert to free trade.[4] Whether the U.S. government's intervention makes the American economy better off, then, depends upon how the foreign government will respond—something that U.S. policymakers can only guess at in advance.

In this world of strategic trade, all sorts of measures that defy the traditional wisdom suddenly make sense. What if there's a promising new technology that researchers from many countries are rushing to develop and exploit? The company that gets the jump on the new technology will have at least a temporary monopoly and with it the ability to obtain monopoly profits from foreign customers. Since it would reap large profits, the company itself would seem to have strong incentives to do the optimal amount of research and development on its own. But faced with the possibility that some foreign firm may jump into the fray with the limitless financial backing of its government, a privately owned company may hesitate. Its own government can help: by intervening to help subsidize the firm's R & D and thus speed up the pace of research, the government can help the domestic firm get its products to market first. Government participation may also deter would-be competitors, assuring the domestic firm a larger share of the world market. The net result may be that the profits of the domestic firm rise by more than the amount of the subsidy, increasing the country's total income.

Thus, government intervention in what appears to be a private business decision can make the country better off. On the other hand, if the government chooses not to act and some foreign government moves to subsidize *its* firm, the foreigners may succeed in obtaining a monopoly and forcing the rest of the world to pay monopoly prices to them.[5]

Government activities that otherwise seem wasteful sometimes make good economic sense when this sort of strategic interplay is considered. Four European governments, for example, have put their resources into Airbus Industrie, a jointly owned firm that manufactures large airplanes. So far, the company's sales revenues have been less than the costs of designing, building, and marketing its planes. In traditional accounting terms, that means that the company "loses money." But its losses are not necessarily an indication that it is inefficient for European governments to subsidize an aircraft manufacturer. After all, there are only two other major manufacturers of commercial jets, both based in the United States. If Airbus Industrie were not in business, that duopoly would probably be able to command substantially higher prices for airplanes. The very existence of Airbus Industrie weakens the other two firms' hold on the market, driving down the price of airplanes. The competition among manufacturers allows airlines in the countries that own Airbus Industrie to purchase planes more cheaply than they otherwise could, improving the economic welfare of the countries concerned. One cannot evaluate whether government intervention in the airplane business is economically wise without comparing these savings due to increased competition among airplane manufacturers with the amount of government subsidies the company receives.

Tariffs, quotas, and subsidies are almost always undesirable in the eyes of classical economic theorists. By artificially raising prices in the importing country they reduce consumer welfare, and by distorting the relative prices of various goods they lead purchasers to make decisions that are economically inefficient. In a world of monopolistic competition, on the other hand, protecting the domestic market with tariffs and quotas may make good economic sense. Under free trade, a Japanese manufacturer of videocassette recorders, with few direct competitors, may be able to exploit consumers in the United States by charging prices above the market-clearing level. American companies that want to make the same product may be unable to get off the ground because the Japanese firm's large production allows it to produce each unit more cheaply than a newcomer with a small production run can do; the established firm will be able to offer its recorders at lower prices and still make a profit. A tariff or a quota could materially change the situation by *increasing* competition, raising the foreigner's prices so the newcomer could be cost-competitive. Once the domestic company is able to compete, the tariff could be withdrawn.

In the short run, the domestic economy might be worse off due to the higher prices caused by the tariff. In the long run, however, it will benefit for two different reasons. First, while competition will remain imperfect and both firms will make high profits, a share of the profits that previously went abroad to shareholders of the foreign firm will now remain in the domestic economy. Second, domestic prices are likely to be lower with two competitors in the running than when there was just one.[6] And once a certain amount of competition is established, the government can use its ability to regulate imports and subsidize exports to disrupt any attempt at collusion or price fixing, either by encouraging still more firms to enter the market or by keeping the foreigners from being able to count on maintaining a certain slice of the market.[7]

The case for government involvement becomes even more convincing if expertise in producing one product is critical to producing another. Makers of computer memory chips, for example, typically entered the business by making relatively simple 4K dynamic random access memories. In doing so, they learned to master the design and production techniques required for the denser 16K chips, the second generation of DRAMs. Those chips in turn proved to be stepping-stones to production of the far more complex 64K chips. At each stage of chip development, the increasing costs of research and production and the evidence of sustained, well-financed foreign competition will drive some competitors from the market. That decision to exit is irreversible: companies that did not make 64K chips were, practically speaking, unable to compete in the 256K chip market.

From the point of view of a national government, a domestic

company's decision to drop out at any point means elimination from the competition forever, leaving foreigners in control of the market and, perhaps, in a position to extract monopoly profits in the future. If domestic companies persist in the semiconductor business, on the other hand, they not only keep the foreigners from obtaining a monopoly but they themselves may be able to achieve strong international market power in the future, allowing them to exploit foreign markets. A program of protection, tax breaks, or direct government subsidies to bolster domestic companies' positions at an early point in the industry's development will clearly be a net cost to the economy in the short run, but over the long run it may be repaid many times over if the domestically owned companies succeed in maintaining their positions in the market. The difficulty lies in calculating exactly when such a program of government support is economically efficient, an issue that economists are just beginning to address.[8]

Many high-tech products also have another characteristic that creates a role for government intervention in cases where there is a potential for monopoly profits. Goods such as telephone equipment and computers are generally most useful as part of a network, so a customer considering whether to purchase a certain type of computer must consider the number of other people likely to buy equipment compatible with his. The value of the computer will be reduced if few other people purchase equipment with which it can communicate, and it will be enhanced if the computer proves able to use a broad range of software, to interact with numerous commercial databases and to send data to many other computers. The expected number of total customers for the product is important in each potential customer's purchase decision. Individual firms, however, may not take account of these network effects in their production decisions. If the government subsidizes a domestic firm's computer sales in its home country, that will raise the firm's output and lead to greater expectations about the total number of units to be sold. Those greater expectations of network size, in turn, will lead to increased sales both at home and abroad, giving the domestic firm an international competitive advantage against its foreign competitors and capturing for the domestic economy the excess profits available in imperfectly competitive foreign markets. The result could be a net gain in national income—unless foreign competitors retaliate by offering similar subsidies to their producers.[9]

Is free trade still desirable? For the world as a whole, the answer turns out to be usually but not always. In most cases, even with imperfect competition, the total global output of goods and services will be greatest if everything can be traded freely and if every country makes those things it produces most efficiently. Free trade will allow a single factory in any country to turn out goods at the most efficient level of production, even if that level is too high for its national market, and will thus help keep costs down. At the same time, free trade ensures a flow of goods that will make it harder for a domestic producer to maintain a monopoly at the expense of domestic consumers. The prices of goods and services will eventually equalize throughout the world, so that production and consumption in every country will be shaped according to the true cost of labor, capital, and raw materials—the economic recipe for efficiency.[10]

If, however, there is truly a worldwide monopoly or even an oligopoly controlling the production of a specific good or service, free trade may not be best. By protecting its own market, a country can encourage formation of a new firm that would eventually compete with the monopoly or oligopoly not only at home but abroad as well. The more companies there are in competition, the more difficult it will be for them to agree to divide up the market and charge high prices. The world as a whole, then, will benefit from lower prices and a more competitive environment. The home countries of the companies that previously controlled the market may end up in a worse position because the flow of monopoly profits will diminish, but total world income and output are bound to increase.

For an individual country, the case for interference with free trade in some specific product is even stronger. There are many countries in which only foreigners market cars, computers, and videocassette recorders under circumstances of imperfect competition. They provide few jobs and little income, steadily extracting the country's wealth in the form of excessive profits and sending it abroad. In theory, proper government intervention could either increase competition or, at the least, extract a share of the profits for use in the domestic economy rather than letting those profits flow unrestricted to foreign stockholders.

In practice, however, it's hard to know when the government's interference with free trade will serve to increase a nation's income rather than to reduce economic welfare. The cases in which government intervention is justifiable in theoretical terms, such as those outlined here, are difficult to identify quickly enough to make intervention useful, and individual firms have strong incentives to ask for government aid even when those conditions are not met. Some advocates of systematic government policies to aid key industries have put forth simple tests, such as targeting industries that have the highest value added per worker or the strongest linkages with other sectors of the economy.[11] But those criteria have often proved counterproductive. Protecting industries with the highest value added per worker simply channels resources to the firms that are most capital-intensive, such as chemical companies and oil refineries, regardless of whether encouraging even stronger capital intensity is economically efficient. Nor does the fact that an industry offers linkages with other sectors necessarily mean that greater investment in that industry is desirable. In addition, if there are only a few firms in the domestic industry, protecting them from foreign competitors could allow them to establish an oligopoly and force up prices, much to the country's economic detriment.

Even if we assume that a strong case for interference with free trade exists, the new trade theory as yet offers little guidance as to exactly how the government can best intervene. Would an import tariff accomplish the purpose better than a direct subsidy to the producer? How much of a subsidy should be offered? How high a quota is required? So far, economics has been unable to give answers in individual cases. It may never be able to, because most types of intervention have undesired side effects, such as encouraging the formation of inefficient new companies that then lobby for protection to be extended indefinitely. And, of course, once companies start lining up for relief, it becomes difficult for administrators and politicians to distinguish between cases where some form of government involvement will increase the economy's efficiency and cases where government action will make the economy worse

off. Notes economist Paul Krugman, one of the pioneers in building
the theoretical case for government intervention in trade matters,
"There is a theoretical case for industrial targeting. A time may
come when economists are sufficiently knowledgeable to make concrete policy recommendations based on that theoretical case. As it
stands now, however, the theory does not look very operational."[12]

In recent years, the increasing internationalization of the ownership of capital has added yet more complications to this calculus.
A large proportion of world trade now consists of intracorporate
transactions—shipments from one subsidiary of a transnational
corporation to another. A government's measures that interfere with
imports are likely also to interfere with the production and distribution patterns of locally based companies, possibly reducing their
domestic employment and their profitability and thus rendering the
country worse off. In addition, many of the potential gains from
government action come from redirecting monopoly profits from
stockholders of a "foreign" firm to owners of a "domestic" one.
With relatively open international capital markets, however, a "foreign" firm may well have many "domestic" citizens as its shareholders. If government intervention hurts the "foreign" firm in such
a case, the "domestic" stockholders will be harmed as well, while
foreign citizens, to the extent that they own shares in a "domestic"
company, will end up benefiting from government policies specifically intended to keep profits from going to foreigners.

Most critically of all, a government cannot intervene in international trade wisely unless it can predict how its trading partners
will respond. An action that promises great economic advantages
when considered in isolation will usually look far less promising if
retaliation is likely. Even when the trading partner decides not to
strike back immediately, a step taken by one country that effectively
hurts another is likely to poison future relations, diminishing the
chances of cooperation in the future and making everybody worse
off in the long run. And while any country may be able to improve
its lot by interfering with free trade in some particular good, the
calculus may look very different if other countries take similar steps
with regard to other products, destroying the general principle of
unrestricted trade that undergirds the world trading system.

The message of the new trade policy, then, is that wise government intervention in the international flow of goods and services is a complicated business. In an industry featuring a large number of competitors around the world turning out similar or identical products such as textiles, shoes, or petrochemicals, there is little opportunity to reap above-normal profits from foreigners. In that case, no type of government intervention will make the economy better off under any circumstances, despite promises that it will "save jobs." If the industry is or promises to become a monopoly or a tight oligopoly and another country has already intervened on behalf of one of its firms, on the other hand, carefully planned government action to help a domestic firm gain a share of the extra-high profits may be desirable—provided the government believes that foreigners are unlikely to retaliate.[13]

By defining so narrowly the circumstances under which government intervention in trade will improve a country's economic welfare, the new trade theory in no way supports political demands for protection from import competition. Instead, by emphasizing the strategic response of one nation's government to the actions of another, it offers a warning: if governments do not create ongoing means of promoting and enforcing cooperation in international trade, nations' attempts to use trade policy to extract economic advantage from one another threaten to make the entire world poorer.

9

Antitrust Reconsidered

C apitalism poses a paradox. Struggling against one another to survive and prosper, people and companies ceaselessly invent new products, new ways of exploiting nature, new methods of making their operations more profitable. For society, that competition is to the good, because the wealth it generates means improved standards of living. But for individual businesses, intense competition means low prices and low profits. Monopoly, and with it the ability to extract extrahigh returns from the investment of time, labor, and money, is every capitalist's dream.

Governments in capitalist countries, then, face a fundamental problem. By interfering with private business arrangements, they may hamper efficiency and retard the creation of new economic wealth. But by failing to interfere, they encourage moves that curtail competition, such as cartels and price-fixing agreements. Those moves too cause inefficiency and a loss in social welfare. Distinguishing between the cases when government intervention will increase competition and when it will reduce competition is rarely easy. It may take years or decades to tell whether a given merger, a joint research project, or a cooperative marketing arrangement eventually results in a less competitive economy—and by then, if competition has been diminished, it will likely be too late to bring it back. The antitrust authorities must decide whether to intervene in individual cases without knowing what would occur were they to reach a different decision.

For precisely that reason, economics played little role in antitrust enforcement until the latter years of the 1970s. The classic economic case against monopoly was well understood, of course: to maximize profits, a monopolist will set output below what it would be under competitive conditions. This reduced supply will allow him to obtain a higher price for each unit he sells, enhancing his own welfare but reducing the overall welfare of society. Other allegedly anticompetitive actions, such as a manufacturer's rule barring its "independent" dealers from selling goods made by competitors, were suspect on the grounds that they too would allow businesses eventually to stifle competition and jack up prices. But in individual cases of antitrust enforcement, there was rarely an attempt to explain in rigorous economic terms exactly why the conduct under challenge would make society worse off. Courts routinely blocked mergers and acquisitions merely because they would increase the concentration of economic resources, without showing that the company in question would be able to exercise market power and raise prices above the free market level.

In one famous 1966 case, the U.S. Supreme Court blocked the merger of two Los Angeles grocery chains although the two combined would have controlled only 7.5 percent of the local grocery market. Antitrust law, the court ruled, was intended to "prevent economic concentration in the American economy by keeping a large number of small competitors in business," and the question of whether consumers would have suffered harm from the merger was irrelevant.[1] A year later, a large consumer products company, Procter & Gamble, was barred from buying a bleach manufacturer. The court specifically refused to consider arguments that the deal might increase operating efficiency and lower prices for consumers; instead, it reasoned that Procter & Gamble's large size and advertising budgets might give the bleach company an unfair advantage against competitors.[2] Perhaps the most extreme case of incomprehensible antitrust enforcement came in 1969, when the Justice Department sought to block three acquisitions by the International Telephone and Telegraph Company even though ITT was not in a position to monopolize any of the industries involved. The problem, the government alleged, was simply that ITT was too big. As a conglomerate, it might be able to force suppliers to buy from one of its units in order to be allowed to sell to some other unit, although there was no evidence that such things had ever occurred. After two years of litigation, the company and the government reached a settlement requiring ITT to sell several businesses and barring it from acquiring any large American company for ten years without government approval—regardless of whether the acquisition would cause problems of a competitive nature.[3]

Some business practices, such as attempts by manufacturers to set the prices at which retailers sell their products, were defined by Congress and the courts to be illegal per se, no matter what reasonable justification they might have. Others, such as tying (a requirement that a customer purchase one product or service in order to purchase another), were usually enough to trigger an antitrust suit. Clear, economically sound explanations of who would be harmed by such objectionable actions were rarely to be found.

As the winds of laissez-faire economics swept through academia in the 1970s, economists and law professors offered a withering critique of traditional antitrust policy. Aaron Director and George J. Stigler, economists at the University of Chicago, were among the first to analyze the effects of antitrust law in formal economic terms. Stigler, for example, showed mathematically in 1964 that looking only at the number of firms in an industry isn't enough to see whether those companies are wielding unhealthy economic power; the relative sizes of the firms, the number of customers, and the entry of new customers are also important in analyzing whether an oligopoly possesses the power to drive up prices.[4] At the University of Chicago Law School and in the economics department, Director and Stigler trained many of the scholars who became influential actors in the antitrust arena in the 1970s and 1980s, establishing what became known as the "law and economics" movement.

Starting from the assumption that the underlying purpose of antitrust law should be to increase economic efficiency, they argued that cases should deal with the basic economic question of whether sellers are able to control price and output, rather than such narrow legal issues as whether a cartel exists. As a general rule, this "Chicago school" contended, businesses' behavior is governed by the desire to maximize profits. One way to achieve that end is to operate as efficiently as possible, and most of the policies and actions businesses adopt are for this purpose. This increase in efficiency is good for the economy as a whole, because if a business uses fewer resources to produce a given amount of its product, that means that more resources are available for other purposes. At the same time, of course, some business practices may result in a particular company or cartel gaining the market power that lets it raise prices. Therefore, law and economics theorists urged, courts should weigh the gains and the losses in deciding whether a particular business arrangement violates the antitrust laws. If the efficiency gains are larger than the potential loss to consumer welfare, then the arrangement is economically beneficial to society and should not be prohibited.[5]

In this view, cartels, monopolies, and oligopolies are often good, because "concentration persists only where it brings efficiencies or is the consequence of superior management."[6] If concentration is not efficient, its presence is not a serious social problem demanding government attention, because prices will not remain above free market levels for long. Cartels and oligopolies tend to be unstable and have a tendency to self-destruct as members cheat on their agreements not to undercut each other on price. In addition, the Chicago school taught, all would-be monopolists and oligopolists must face the fact that if they raise prices too high, the existence of fat profits will attract new competitors to the industry even as it causes consumers to seek substitutes for the expensive products. Because most such attempts to charge extrahigh prices will eventually fail, antitrust enforcement intended to reduce the concentration of ownership in a particular industry rarely brings economic benefit to society.[7]

Perhaps the most telling economic case against traditional antitrust enforcement, however, was the theory of "contestability" developed in the late 1970s by economists working for Bell Telephone Laboratories. Unlike the Chicago school's analysis, contestability theory made no assumptions that private economic arrangements are necessarily efficient. Nor did it require a weighing of the efficiency gains and losses from mergers and acquisitions. Instead, contestability theory emphasized the importance of *potential* rather than actual competition in allowing market forces to work.

At the time, the U.S. Department of Justice was attempting to break up Bell Labs' parent company, the American Telephone and Telegraph Company, after charging AT&T with monopolizing the communications business. AT&T's enormous share of the industry was indisputable, but its economists pointed out that from an economic point of view, a monopoly doesn't necessarily make society worse off. After all, they argued, the only economic reason to worry about a monopoly is that it may be able to restrict output and raise prices. Suppose, however, that potential competitors—other long-distance telephone companies, for example—are ready to jump into the business whenever prices rise. If those firms can enter the industry easily without making investments that would be unrecoverable if they later exit, the monopolist will lose its monopoly if it attempts to raise prices. Hence, the argument went, the sole trucking company serving a given route has strong incentives not to exercise its monopoly power to raise rates, because other truckers could quickly shift their vehicles to that route with very little unrecoverable expense. At the extreme, if a market is perfectly contestable and newcomers can enter with no cost whenever prices are above free market levels, a monopolist will price its product exactly as a competitive firm would and there will be no harm to society. Before bringing an antitrust case, then, the government should consider not only the number of firms in an industry but also the degree to which the industry is contestable.[8] This argument, expressed in simple but elegant mathematical terms, unleashed a veritable flood of theoretical and empirical research examining the implications of contestability for the enforcement of antitrust law.

Parallel to these arguments for the relaxation of traditional antimonopoly enforcement, economists with a free market orientation advocating the "new antitrust economics" were also developing a more formal analysis of other business practices that generations of lawyers had come to label "anticompetitive." If a firm chooses to establish certain business policies, they contended, that might well be because those policies are simply efficient ways to operate. A company's decision to integrate vertically by buying its supplier firms or its customers, for example, was alleged to eliminate many of the risks involved in transacting business with an outside firm of uncertain reliability; even if they do not directly lower production costs, such acquisitions may reduce the amount of money the firm spends on legal fees and insurance to protect itself against its business partners, which are an unproductive use of resources. The federal prohibition on resale price maintenance—the practice by which manufacturers set the prices at which retailers must sell their products—came under sharp attack on the grounds that price maintenance does not reduce output or increase prices but rather allows manufacturers to maintain customer satisfaction. Price maintenance, the argument went, enables retailers to provide a high level of service and information without worrying that customers will then go to a cheaper, low-service store to make their purchases; without such assurance, retailers would have less incentive to provide service and information, and sales of the manufacturer's products would suffer.

Legal rulings against many other once common practices—tying and reciprocal dealing arrangements; contracts in which the dealer must agree to handle only the goods of one manufacturer exclusively; vertical market division, in which a manufacturer limits its distributors to selling in a specific geographic area; refusals to deal with a potential customer in an effort to exercise monopoly power—all came under similarly sharp attack from free market theorists. In all cases, the basic argument was the same: rarely, if ever, does the enforcement of such policies allow a manufacturer to exercise monopoly power and raise prices. For its most ardent proponents, the "new antitrust economics" allowed for only one type of business arrangement so pernicious that it could have no economic justification: the out-and-out price-fixing ring.[9]

In the United States, the teachings of the Chicago school quickly became the antitrust dogma of the Reagan administration, starting in 1981. Each of the three directors of the Department of Justice's Antitrust Division under Reagan was a firm believer in restrained enforcement of the antitrust laws. Both in the Justice Department and at the Federal Trade Commission, which is also involved in antitrust enforcement, officials repeatedly emphasized that sound economic analysis would be the cornerstone of antitrust policy, replacing the less scientific approach of years past.

Claiming that recent economic research had made the Department of Justice's 1968 guidelines on mergers "no longer appropriate," the Antitrust Division and the FTC formed working groups of economists and attorneys to develop new standards for determining which mergers and acquisitions the government should challenge. In place of the traditional practice of objecting to any merger that would result in a single firm's having a large share of the market for a certain product within a given geographic area, the FTC adopted a new approach in 1982. Rather than looking at size or market share, the commission said, it would focus on the general characteristics of the industry in question, including such things as entry barriers, technological change, changes in demand for the industry's products, and the presence of firms in nearby geographic markets that might enter the market under study. In particular, the commission expressed reluctance to block mergers in newly developing industries or in industries that are undergoing major technological change, because "market power . . . may be harder to exercise or less likely to endure in the face of rapid technological change or significant upward shifts in demand." Even if a merger were thought to have anticompetitive effects, the FTC might allow it to proceed on grounds of efficiency, given "substantial evidence that the resulting cost savings could not have been obtained without the merger and clearly outweigh any increase in market power." For the first time—albeit with some hesitation—economic considerations of efficiency found a role in antitrust policy.[10]

The Justice Department's own merger guidelines, issued in 1984, brought the Chicago school's economic approach even more strongly to bear. In evaluating a proposed merger, the department said, it would study each product produced or sold by the merging firms and analyze economically what would occur if a hypothetical monopolist of that product tried to raise prices. If, in the Justice Department's opinion, a price increase would cause so many buyers to switch to substitute products that the monopolist would lose money (that is, in economic terms, if price elasticity of demand were high), then the government should not worry if one firm gains control of a large share of that market. Similarly, if the price rise would allow other firms to begin making the product within one year, or if it would cause firms in other geographic areas to enter the market in question, the merger would be viewed less seriously. In other words, an economic determination as to the contestability of the market became part of the Justice Department's analysis. Even if a merger was judged likely to harm competition, the department might approve it if the parties could show that it would lead to efficiencies, ranging from economies of scale in production to reduced transportation costs and lower overhead expenses. The rationale for that position, the guidelines stated, was that "the primary benefit of mergers to the economy is their efficiency-enhancing potential, which can increase the competitiveness of firms and result in lower prices to consumers."[11]

In addition to reshaping merger policy along the lines proposed by free market theorists, the Justice Department loosened the standards for the types of "vertical" arrangements companies at different levels of an industry could make without violating antitrust laws. In 1983 the Antitrust Division asked the U.S. Supreme Court to overturn seventy-one years of case law flatly prohibiting price maintenance and to rule that no vertical restraints should be flatly illegal. The high court, however, politely declined the invitation.[12]

Two years later, the Department of Justice issued guidelines indicating that it would not object to many types of vertical arrangements that had run afoul of previous attorneys general. For example, price maintenance would be attacked in court only when a manufacturer and its distributors had agreed "as to the specific prices" to be charged; a general agreement between a manufacturer and a dealer to maintain prices without mentioning a specific dollar figure would not be objectionable. If a group of dealers were to allocate customers among themselves and obtain the manufacturer's concurrence, the department said they would be treated the same as if the manufacturer had initiated the process as a harmless vertical restraint, a position that ignored several Supreme Court decisions restricting cooperation among dealers of a single brand. A manufacturer's attempt to "tie" the sale of two products would not trigger objections so long as the Justice Department believed "the economic advantages of jointly packaging and merchandising two different products are substantial," again applying an economic test to a practice that was previously viewed with the utmost suspicion. Exclusive dealing—a seller's attempt to force a buyer not to buy from anyone else—was viewed in a similar light.[13]

Finally, the Reagan Justice Department proposed in 1986 to revise the nation's antitrust laws, because "the body of economic learning upon which antitrust enforcement policy and judicial doctrine regarding mergers is based has changed substantially." The proposed changes to Section 7 of the Clayton Act, an antitrust law enacted in 1914, provided that a merger would be illegal only if there is a "significant probability" that it will harm competition, a far tighter standard than the existing language barring mergers that "tend to" reduce competition. Such harm would have been evidenced solely by the power to raise prices profitably above competitive levels for a significant period of time, rather than by any measurement of the market share the merged company would control. Most importantly, the bill attempted to enshrine the "law and economics" movement in federal law by directing courts to consider all relevant economic factors, including potential efficiencies, in deciding whether to block a merger.[14] Congress, which found these legal changes highly objectionable, refused to approve the bill.

Basing antitrust policy on economic considerations is a simple idea. But merging law and economics turns out to be a difficult undertaking. Though the Reagan administration ordered in 1986 that all potential antitrust cases first be reviewed by economists to determine whether the conduct involved would truly reduce competition, making such a determination with precision is an impossibility. Faced with the challenge in a particular case, Justice Department economists would do rough calculations of the loss in consumer welfare stemming from a proposed merger by estimating how much prices would increase as the industry became more concentrated, and would then forecast the efficiency gains from the merger based on existing economic studies of the industry in question. If both sets of figures were accurate, a comparison of the gains and the losses was used to indicate whether the case made economic sense and should be pursued. But as the Antitrust Division's chief economist commented in 1986, "I don't think we can do very accurate estimates. Plus or minus fifty percent ain't bad." After all, efficiency tests are only as good as the numbers they evaluate, and the numbers are generally not much good at all.[15]

Aside from the practical difficulties of determining which activities are economically efficient, the economic theories of the law and economics movement are far less robust than its proponents acknowledge. Although the Reagan administration's Justice Department has claimed to have economic truth on its side in relaxing restraints on business conduct, the economic precepts that underpin its theories are open to serious challenge. In many cases, those free market theories are based on very special assumptions that rarely prevail in the real world.

Take, for example, the theory of contestability. The assertion that potential competition can keep prices low even in markets with few actual competitors has powerfully affected antitrust policy. It played a prominent role in the government's decision not to oppose any of the numerous mergers in the airline industry between 1984 and 1987. Commercial aviation was supposedly a primary example of a contestable industry, since the airlines' "capital with wings" could easily be shifted among routes if lack of competition on any individual route caused fares to rise. Under that assumption, it made little difference that the purchase of Republic Airlines by Northwest Orient Airlines left Northwest with a near-monopoly on service to Minneapolis; some other carrier, seeing the enormous profits to be made, would bully its way into the market, forcing prices down.

But commercial aviation turned out to be not so contestable as opponents of government intervention believed.[16] Every sizable airline adopted a strategy of building "hubs" at which its flights connect, and those hubs have proved to be important barriers to the entry of new airlines. Creating a hub involves large sunk costs for such things as marketing and construction of terminals. A newcomer would have to incur similar costs that it could not recover if it later decided to pull out. Furthermore, the very fact that one carrier has gone to such expense is a sign that it plans to stay and fight for the market, so the investment itself works to deter would-be competitors. Finally, if one airline offers a network of flights into a single hub, a newcomer can hardly expect to compete by offering just a handful, and the need to enter the market in a major way may dissuade many potential competitors from entering at all. As a result, many airlines have been able to maintain monopolies on individual routes for long periods of time, and fares per mile on those routes are far higher than on routes with competition. Profits have not equalized among the routes, as should be the case if aviation is truly contestable.[17]

Of course, no industry is completely contestable. A business entering any new market must make investments that it will not be able to recover should it later decide to pull out. Promotional materials and price lists must be prepared. Advertisements must be targeted at the new customer base. A new distribution system must be established. Contracts must be written, and personnel must be relocated. Even if no new physical plant is required, these sorts of sunk costs are inevitable.

Firms already in the market, having already incurred the sunk costs required to participate, can always inflict unrecoverable costs on newcomers by such means as setting prices below the cost of production, forcing the new firm to lose money on each unit it sells. (Although the existing firms will also lose money, they do so in the knowledge that they will return to profitability as soon as the newcomer withdraws.) This possibility was not considered in early work on contestability, but it turns out to have enormous importance in explaining why potential competition does not keep prices down as well as actual competition. Although a market may superficially appear to be contestable, every market has barriers that can deter new firms from entering and allow existing firms to extract excess profits. The threat of entry may keep those profits smaller than if prices were at monopoly levels, but profits will still be higher than under perfect competition, and consumers will still be worse off.[18]

Contestability remains a useful theoretical construct and is helpful in cases where regulatory agencies must approve prices, but it is of limited use in determining whether or not a given merger will end up reducing overall economic welfare. In any case, it provides little support for the Reagan administration's assertions that low barriers to entry in an industry will keep the firms already in the industry from charging excessive prices, or that prices set above competitive levels cannot endure for long. As the fathers of contestability theory wrote angrily in 1986, "Contestability theory does not, and was not intended to, lend support to those who believe (or almost seem to believe) that the unrestrained market automatically solves all economic problems. . . . Before anyone can legitimately use the analysis to infer that virtue reigns in some economic sector and that interference is therefore unwarranted, that person must first provide evidence that the arena in question is, in fact, highly contestable."[19]

Just as the Reagan administration's general approval of merger activity is based on the belief that mergers usually increase economic efficiency, its acceptance of vertical restraints depends upon

the assumption that firms manage their conduct primarily to minimize costs. In this view, strongly supported by Chicago school theorists, such policies as resale price maintenance and allocation of
exclusive territories to dealers induce efficiency. Suppose XYZ Corporation, a manufacturer, depends upon retailers to deliver essential
services, such as promotion, repair, credit, and sales effort, as they
sell XYZ's product. If these services are provided, they may increase
demand for the product, so it is in XYZ's interest that dealers offer
them. But unless XYZ can assure dealers that they will be able to
incorporate the cost of those services into their prices, dealers will
have no incentive to provide them, because otherwise low-price,
low-service competitors will force prices down. To solve the problem, XYZ may insist that no store sell its product for less than the
recommended price, or it may achieve the same end by guaranteeing
each retailer the exclusive right to sell the product in a geographic
area. Those methods purportedly ensure that the proper amount of
service is provided and thus keep XYZ's distribution network operating efficiently.[20] Similarly, a retailer might not adequately advertise a product without the exclusive right to sell it, because
otherwise its ads will benefit other stores selling the same good.
This lack of advertising reduces total sales, diminishing the manufacturer's profit. By using vertical restraints to assure retailers that
they will not lose sales to free-riding stores that refuse to advertise,
the manufacturer makes its sales network more efficient and increases its own profits.[21]

These restraints, according to economists opposing government
intervention, almost never harm consumers, because consumers are
free to buy some competing good if a manufacturer's practices drive
up the price of its products. Indeed, such Chicago school theorists
as Richard Posner and Robert Bork, both of whom were appointed
federal appeals court judges by President Reagan, have argued that
vertical restraints ought to be declared legal in all cases. If a restraint
is economically inefficient, they argue, profits will decline and the
practice will eventually be abandoned. Only under unusual circumstances, such as when a small number of manufacturers dominate
a market and they all use resale price maintenance effectively to fix
retail prices, would they recommend that the government challenge
the practice.

Vertical restraints, however, are not so benign as this laissez-faire analysis would have it. Although restraints may induce retailers to provide a higher level of service and information, some customers may be well informed and not desire the information. They are forced to pay extra for services that are useless to them. Perhaps they could buy a competing product at a lower price, but that's not likely. After all, if some other manufacturer sells a product very similar to XYZ Corporation's widget, XYZ will face the same free-rider problems with its competitors' dealers as it feared among its own: customers could go to XYZ's full-service retailers for information, then buy the cheaper substitute elsewhere. XYZ's efforts to keep the retail price of its product high thus imply that there are no good substitutes. And in that case, XYZ is effectively maintaining a monopoly. The manufacturer maximizes its profits, but consumers buy less of the good than they otherwise would and pay more for it. The economy is better off only in the odd case that many consumers benefit from the "free" information full-service dealers provide and relatively few are forced to buy information they do not desire.[22] Other approaches to achieve the same end, such as sharing the cost of advertising between retailers and manufacturers, would be far less harmful to competition.

Vertical restraints can be undesirable for another reason as well: a company can use them strategically to deter competitors. Take, for example, a manufacturer's insistence that its dealers not carry competitors' products, the practice known in legal circles as "exclusive dealing." On the surface, this seems like a reasonable way for the manufacturer to make sure that the retailer devotes full attention to selling its goods rather than some competitor's. At the same time, however, exclusive dealing can have a strongly anticompetitive effect. A new manufacturer trying to sell air conditioners may find that the existing air conditioner dealers all have exclusive arrangements with one manufacturer or another; none of them can carry the new products. The newcomer will be unable to break into the market unless it sets up a separate dealer network of its own. The costs of doing so may force it to set its prices so high that consumers will not buy the product.[23] If that happens, exclusive dealerships will have had the effect of reducing competition.

The Reagan administration's claims that vertical restraints are generally harmless failed to consider these strategic aspects of business behavior. Though they may have legitimate business purposes, most vertical restraints can also be used in a deliberate effort to raise rivals' costs and to erect barriers to the entry of new competitors.[24] Labeling them acceptable without fully investigating their potential uses as strategic weapons to reduce competition is hardly an example of antitrust policy based on sound economic analysis.

At first glance, introducing an economic calculus into antitrust enforcement seems a logical and praiseworthy step. The claim that the U.S. government can use the scientific principles of economics to adopt antitrust policies that are best at fostering competition and efficiency, however, is less an indication of wisdom than a sign of hubris. In reality, economists have no useful general prescriptions for making the economy more efficient. Many of the common assertions used to justify government nonintervention in the antitrust arena are simply wrong.

Even the most standard economic assumption, that competition results in more efficient allocation of resources than does monopoly, is not correct in all cases. Take the case of an industry such as plastics, where extremely high capital investments are required before anything is produced. If the government encourages competition (by, for example, dropping a requirement that firms obtain permits to produce plastics), the industry's leading firms may respond strategically by deliberately building excess production capacity to warn potential competitors away. Any firm considering a move into the plastics industry will be aware that if it enters, other companies have the capacity to increase output quickly and drive prices so low that the business will be unprofitable. But unless the new firms enter, the capacity sits unused, representing a waste of resources. It may even be the case that the economic cost to society of building and maintaining that unused capacity exceeds the cost of the anticompetitive practices that existed before the government moved to encourage competition.

Or look at an issue debated by antitrust experts for decades, price discrimination: should manufacturers be allowed to sell their goods to large buyers at lower prices than small buyers pay? The law prohibiting the practice, the Robinson-Patman Act, was passed with the aim of protecting small business from having to pay higher prices. Many economists have criticized the law and asserted that price discrimination is economically efficient, allowing the manufacturer to reduce prices to some buyers without raising prices for others. But that conclusion depends strongly upon assumptions about how buyers will respond to the seller's pricing decision and about the nature of the products in question. For partially finished goods being sold from one manufacturer to others, price discrimination may reduce economic welfare in some situations and improve it in others—and, in advance, there is no simple way to know.[25]

Because of uncertainty about the ways in which companies will compete in a dynamic world, economic models are simply unable to draw far-reaching conclusions about what improves economic welfare and what reduces it. In any given case, the specifics of the situation make all the difference: How many potential entrants are there? Are they able to enter quickly enough to establish themselves before existing firms counterattack? If one enters, will others enter or remain on the sidelines? Do the existing firms compete by making production decisions in advance, or do they constantly adjust output after observing each others' actions? Will they all seek to deter newcomers, or will some break ranks? Will an increased number of firms necessarily mean lower prices? How will the changing number of firms affect the amount of research and development each one does? The answers to many of these questions are impossible to know before an event takes place, yet without them stock economic theories become hopelessly irrelevant.[26]

In many individual cases, then, economics has surprisingly little to say about whether a proposed merger, a company's distribution strategy, or a company's policies on pricing will be good or bad for the economy. Economic theory provides a strong framework within which government officials can ask questions before deciding whether to intervene, but it offers few concrete answers. It certainly does not demonstrate, as believers in laissez-faire assert, that the best antitrust policy for the economy is one in which the government does not interfere. In the end, officials dealing with an antitrust case must still rely on their own judgments about the likely course of future events, predicting as best they can the ways in which their decisions will shape future patterns of competition. Although some economists would pretend that economic science has rendered such fallible human judgments unnecessary, there are no easy, automatic answers.

10
That Puzzling Business Cycle

T he business cycle is one of the constants of modern life. In the popular conception, the economy is a roller coaster, endlessly moving up and down in a cyclical pattern, from peaks of strong growth and low unemployment to troughs of painful depression and back again. As Arthur F. Burns, a pathbreaking scholar of economic fluctuations, wrote in 1947: "For well over a century, business cycles have run an unceasing round. They have persisted through vast economic and social changes; they have withstood countless experiments in industry, agriculture, banking, industrial relations, and public policy; they have confounded forecasters without number, belied repeated prophecies of a 'new era of prosperity' and outlived repeated forebodings of 'chronic depression.'"[1]

When economists and politicians talk of "stabilizing the economy," what they are really discussing is leveling out these economic swings. Reducing economic fluctuations would be no mean achievement: if the economy were more stable, the unemployment rate would not jump up and down, factories would not face surplus capacity one year and a backlog of orders the next, and almost everyone would feel more secure about his or her economic future. The misery experienced by millions of people in the depths of depression would be eliminated. Some economists even believe that having fewer economic ups and downs will lead to a higher average rate of economic growth over the long term, which would make almost everyone better off.[2]

For five decades, how to deal with the business cycle has been the basic issue dividing activist economists from those of a more classical bent. The basic belief that has defined an "activist," in fact, has been the faith that economic stabilization is both possible and desirable. To accomplish that, these believers in constant government efforts to tame the business cycle would enlist both monetary and fiscal policies to stimulate the economy during downturns and restrain it during booms with a view to keeping the growth rate steady. Economists opposed to activist economic policies have taken the opposite position, holding that cyclical fluctuations lie beyond the ability of government to control. Many economists of that persuasion, including monetarists such as Milton Friedman and rational expectationists such as Robert Lucas, believe that government attempts to make business cycles less extreme can only end up by making them worse. They would argue that the natural tendency of an economy is toward a situation in which all of its capital and labor are employed in the most efficient way possible, and that government intervention interferes with the private decisions about how much of those resources to use. Other economists falling into the small-government camp would concede a role for government intervention in the depths of a long depression but contend that monetary and fiscal policies cannot be used to even out less extreme cyclical swings without triggering unhealthy inflationary pressures.

According to the reckoning of the National Bureau of Economic Research, a private organization that sponsors economic studies, there have been eight full business cycles in the United States since World War II. Although the average period of growth has been just under four years long, individual expansions have been as brief as one year (1980–81) and as long as nine years (1961–69). Economic contractions have been far more uniform, varying in length from six to sixteen months. On average, industrial production drops almost 10 percent during a recession in the United States but rises by one-third during the expansion that follows. Since World War II, recessions have usually resulted in a 3 percentage point rise in unemployment. Expansions, on the other hand, have caused unemployment to fall by only 2 percentage points on average, which obviously means that the unemployment rate has tended to rise over the decades since the war. There is also evidence that the distribution of income becomes more uneven during downturns and improves during periods of growth.[3]

Cycles of this sort are not just an American phenomenon. Other countries experience economic fluctuations as well. Cycles seem to be a universal pattern, occurring regardless of the details of a country's economic system. There is ample evidence that booms and depressions are transmitted from one economy to another through changes in the demand for imports.

Cycles also seem to move in predictable patterns. The first stage is a credit crunch: as the economy is perking prosperously away, businesses want to undertake so many new projects that the demand for credit expands faster than the amount of money people are willing to loan out. Interest rates inevitably rise. Those rising rates quickly lead to lower spending by both companies and households, as it becomes more burdensome to service high-interest debt. People stop buying interest-sensitive goods like houses and automobiles, and businesses put off their investment plans until a time when lower interest rates might make it cheaper to borrow money. Businesses also reduce their inventories to bring them into line with the new, lower levels of demand. Workers' hours are reduced, and some workers are laid off from their jobs. Expansion slows, and the economy may even begin to shrink as a recession occurs.

During the recession, companies bring their inventories into line with their slow sales and then stabilize their buying. At the same time, they typically try to repay their debts to ensure their financial survival as revenues lag. Those two moves mean the worst of the recession is over and the stage is set for recovery. The central bank eases monetary policy so that interest rates can fall. The lower rates make it less costly for businesses to put their money into inventory rather than investing it, so warehouse shelves are gradually restocked. People and businesses begin to borrow again, and companies recall workers to meet the increased demand as the economy improves. Economic confidence returns, and with it a period of prosperity.

The major cause of this endless movement, according to almost all economic theories, is the behavior of interest rates. For decades, therefore, the causes of interest rate fluctuations, and the ability of government to reduce them or to counter their effects, have been the focus of the controversy over whether government intervention in economic affairs can raise the overall level of economic welfare.

On the noninterventionist side, the historical analysis of Milton Friedman and Anna Schwartz found that fluctuations in economic activity in the United States have been accompanied by sharp changes in the growth rate of the money supply affecting both prices and interest rates. This relationship was the basis for their assertion that a steady rate of monetary growth will minimize economic ups and downs. If the economy goes into a slump, they argue, the central bank should not attempt to counteract the downturn by printing money to drive interest rates down because that will only trigger inflation without bringing about any lasting improvement in the economic situation. Nor should the central bank suddenly tighten the money supply if the economy seems to be growing too rapidly because that will lead to a painful deflation. Monetary policy, they contend, is simply not a useful tool for changing the rate of economic growth, so it cannot be used to even out the business cycle.[4]

Rational expectations theory has, like monetarism, accepted monetary instability as the root cause of economic fluctuations, but rational expectationists tell a different story of how that instability affects the economy. They have not accepted the view that high interest rates choke off economic growth. Instead, they contend that unexpected changes in the money supply cause unanticipated changes in prices. Each individual or firm hurriedly tries to adjust its economic actions to the new price level, but it faces a problem: some part of the change in prices may reflect a change in demand for goods or labor, but some unknown part of it is due strictly to inflation. An incorrect guess as to how much the real demand has changed can lead to erroneous business decisions, such as sharp increases or cutbacks in production when smaller changes would have been enough. After taking these misguided steps, of course, firms must make yet more changes in their output and employment in order to bring their production back in line with demand, changes that would never have been necessary had there not been an unanticipated change in the money supply in the first place. The only way to put an end to these fluctuations is to maintain stable economic policies so that people can correctly anticipate and understand changes in prices, supply, and demand.[5]

Keynesians, along with most mainstream economic thinkers today, assert that money supply changes constitute only one of many factors contributing to the repeated tendency to overinvest in times of prosperity. The erratic pattern of consumption and investment behavior, combined with the slowness of wages, employment, and prices in adjusting to economic change, lie at the heart of the Keynesian understanding of the business cycle: people systematically overinvest in times of plenty, leading to a collapse of investment and an ensuing economic decline. In general, Keynesians believe that the central bank can successfully maintain prosperity by loosening the money supply if growth falls below the desired pace and by tightening it if consumers and businesses want to buy more than the country's factories and workers can produce. Many Keynesians, however, contend that monetary policy is more effective at braking a speeding economy than at stimulating a lagging economy. Most of them also assign an important role to the government's fiscal powers, urging that it use tax cuts and spending increases to stimulate the economy during depressions while running budget surpluses to remove excess spending power from the economy during inflationary booms.

These views have become part of the economic mainstream in all industrial countries and have long since ceased to be identified with Keynesians alone. Many economists with a free market orientation but nonmonetarist views also credit monetary policy with the power to regulate the business cycle. What traditionally distinguishes the Keynesians is their belief that the government can also adjust its spending and taxation policies to even out major economic fluctuations. Indeed, Keynes postulated that a boost in government spending, putting more money into individuals' hands to increase the level of consumption, might be the only way to restimulate an economy if conditions become so poor that individuals and businesses are reluctant to make investments no matter how low interest rates fall.

This debate about the proper governmental role in dealing with the business cycle became a staple of economic policy discussions following World War II. There appears to have been a reduction in the seriousness of business downturns over the past five decades, but whether this has been due to more activist government economic policies, to a relative absence of unsettling economic shocks, or to institutional changes that reduce the likelihood of financial panics, such as bank deposit insurance and the separation of banking from investment banking in the United States, remained the focus of controversy until 1982.[6] Then, in a dramatic turn of events, economists Finn E. Kydland of Carnegie-Mellon University and Edward C. Prescott of the University of Minnesota proposed a radical alternative. Neither changes in the money supply nor changes in business investment lie at the heart of the economy's fluctuations, the two economists postulated. Instead, economic swings are precipitated by unforeseen shocks that affect the cost of production, swings on the "real," rather than the financial, side of the economy.

These shocks—a sudden increase in oil prices, the failure of India's monsoons, leading to a drop in world grain output, the appearance of desktop computers to revolutionize office operations—buffet the economy in unexpected ways. If they drive production costs up, they may lead to a period of slow growth or economic decline. But if they result in lower production costs and higher efficiency, the consequence could be a period of prosperity. All, however, affect the ability and willingness of producers to supply goods and services, rather than the desire of customers to purchase them.

The basis for this emphasis on shocks is a series of complicated mathematical models of growth in hypothetical economies that are subjected to sudden changes in the technology of production. By altering nothing but the rate of technological change, Kydland and Prescott showed, these economies can be made to made to fluctuate in patterns similar to those of the U.S. economy. Hence, they conclude, the factors to which economic fluctuations are commonly attributed—changes in the money supply, collapse of financial institutions, excessive investment during good times, leading to surplus capacity—are not required to explain the variations in the rate of economic growth. "Shocks" alone are a sufficient explanation.[7]

A "shock" leads to a change in the rate of economic growth by altering businesses' costs of production, causing them to reassess their plans for future investment. The banking system, guided by the central bank, anticipates these new plans by increasing or decreasing the amount of money it is willing to lend. But because the supply of credit can be changed much more quickly than the supply of manufactured goods or other products that must be physically assembled and shipped, there is a temporary surplus of credit available before the economy begins a growth spurt, and there is a shortage before the beginning of a downturn. In other words, individuals' expectations about the extent and timing of the economic impact of a shock are incorrect. Just as rational expectations theory would have it, these incorrect expectations lead to a temporary state of economic disequilibrium, until individuals have an opportunity to correct their expectations and put the economy back on track. Interest rate changes go hand in hand with economic fluctuations, but they do not *cause* economic movements; it is shocks, not changes in the money supply, that constitute the underlying factor.[8]

This understanding, known as the theory of "real business cycles," suggests that the "business cycle," as understood by generations of economists, is merely a figment of the imagination. Instead of moving up and down in a never-ending cyclical pattern, according to real business cycle theorists, economic fluctuations are completely random, varying around a long-term "trend" rate of growth as one shock after another hits the economy. The fact that the economy is more sluggish this year than last reveals nothing about the prospects for the year to come. There is an equal chance that things will speed up or slow down, so present economic conditions are the best predictor of what lies ahead. Use of the label *cycle* is really just an ill-advised attempt to attribute to these movements a regularity they do not possess, to make us feel that we understand why the economy is behaving as it does. "It's easy to read patterns into data when they're not there," Edward Prescott has observed. "The human mind's pretty inventive."[9]

The assertion that economic fluctuations are random, of course, has extremely strong implications for government policy. If no one can foresee the next shock, it is useless for the government to plan in advance to counteract it. The consequences of any given shock may not be understood until it has come and gone, making a constructive government policy response impossible. Forecasting is out the window. The debate over whether the budget should be in surplus or in deficit loses its importance when no one knows what the economy is likely to do in the future. In fact, active government stabilization policies are likely be counterproductive: if the government expands the budget on the assumption that the economy will be hit by a negative shock but the shock turns out to be be a positive one instead, the result may be far from what the policymakers intended.

In any case, real business cycle theorists argue that fluctuations are generally a good thing for the economy, not a bad thing. From their point of view, economic instability is a necessary part of an economy's painful adjustment to technological change. Trying to keep the economy stable may mean suppressing technological developments, and that, in the long run, may well lead to slower economic growth. Instead of tinkering with measures designed to affect economic performance in the short term, real cycle theorists advise, government policymakers should focus on removing obstacles to long-run economic growth.

The theory is startling. But specifying exactly which shocks have brought about past changes in economic performance has proved a troublesome hurdle for real cycle theorists. The sudden rise of oil prices in 1973 and again in 1979 comes to mind, but it is hard to find another example; the economy fluctuates a great deal, but there are few occasions when the price of a commodity so central to the economy has doubled in so brief a period. Even proponents of real business cycle theory have had difficulty showing that general economic shocks explain much of the historic change in output in individual industries.[10] As an alternative, some have proposed that the economy is buffeted by a constant series of small supply shocks—the sudden invention of a new type of plastic molding machine, an unexpected scarcity of welders—that combine in unpredictable ways. However, small shocks affecting only a single industry are not enough to explain changes in the rate of unemployment throughout the economy.[11] And many major economic trends that have been labeled shocks, such as changes in work force composition as more women enter the workplace, are unlikely to shock anyone since they occur gradually over time rather than suddenly overwhelming a surprised economy.

Shocks certainly explain some economic fluctuations, but they do not explain all of them. There are just too many instances in which other factors—a cut in the money supply, the collapse of important financial institutions, a cutback in government spending—have led to economic decline. The 1981–82 recession in the United States, for example, seems directly traceable to the Federal Reserve Board's decision to curb the rate of money supply growth sharply in 1981. Shocks alone are simply not an adequate explanation, unless one assumes an economy full of frictions, sticky prices, and such slow adjustment to economic change that the effects of a major shock continue to be felt years later—in other words, if one assumes a very Keynesian world far different from the perfect markets that advocates of real business cycle theory take for granted.[12]

Real business cycle theory, then, seems not to answer the long-standing question of what causes economic fluctuations. And if the theory falls short, then its recommendation that the government should pay no attention to the economy's movements loses much of its persuasiveness.

If shocks alone do not cause all of the constant fluctuations in an economy's rate of growth, what else lies behind the business cycle? The long-standing explanations—unstable monetary policy, collapse of financial institutions, triggering a loss of economic confidence, an innate tendency to speculation and overinvestment—do in fact seem to lie at the root of many economic surges and slowdowns. But they are not the whole story. Other factors that often are not even thought of by business cycle analysts may be important contributors to an economy's sudden rise to prosperity or its collapse into depression.

One, surprisingly, is monopoly. An economy in which key markets are served by only one or a small number of producers or distributors seems to be more susceptible to economic downturns than does an economy in which smaller firms prevail. In a healthy economy, the existence of those big companies is often good, because larger firms can do many things more efficiently than smaller ones. But once a recession begins, the relative lack of competition among large firms can turn into an economic drag.

Economists are normally suspicious of monopolies, and with good reason: if a company is the sole seller of a given product and is not regulated by the government, it normally produces less output and sells it for a higher price than it would under more competitive circumstances. A monopolist does not necessarily respond to changes in supply and demand in the same way as competitive firms, by increasing the supply as prices rise and cutting output if prices fall. Instead, if demand for his product rises a monopolist may find that he is better off by reducing output rather than increasing it in order to drive up prices. Falling demand will not necessarily lead the monopolist to reduce output and raise prices; he might be better off turning out more rather than less. For the economy as a whole, these responses will not lead to the greatest possible income, which is why countries with market economies usually have antitrust laws to regulate the behavior of monopolies.

It is relatively rare for privately owned companies to have complete monopoly power. But it is common—and usually legal—for a company to have a monopoly in a narrow product line and compete with other companies that make other products usable for the same purpose. Boeing Corporation, for example, has a monopoly on jet airliners able to carry 450 people, but its monopoly is not total since customers can select somewhat smaller aircraft produced by other companies. Each of those companies also has a monopoly in a particular size range, but it does not have total freedom to set any sale price it wants because customers do have alternatives. Monopolistic competition of this sort is decidedly better for the economy than monopoly, but prices still are generally higher than they would be under perfect competition.

In addition to reducing economic welfare by producing too little, monopolists and monopolistic competitors can make economic downturns worse. Suppose economic growth begins to slow and demand for every company's products falls. Competitive companies would immediately be forced to lower their prices or lose their customers. Monopolists, however, may choose not to cut prices as much as firms in competitive industries, because they can earn more profit with high prices and few sales than they could with lower prices and more sales. If lowering the price would cost money—if it would involve printing up new price lists, putting new price tags on merchandise, or notifying thousands of customers—a monopolist or a monopolistic competitor might actually be better off by not cutting prices at all, even though demand has fallen. But failing to cut prices would bring it even farther away from the level competitive companies would charge, reducing society's economic welfare beyond the harm done by the downturn itself. In effect, the monopolist's inability to change its prices costlessly can make a downturn significantly worse than it otherwise would have been, even if the actual cost of changing those prices is small.

In one sense that's bad. Since most modern economies feature large companies engaging in monopolistic competition in products from computers to specialty chemicals to production machinery, economic downturns may spread farther than in earlier days, when more intense competition was the norm. But in another sense it's good. A central bank's efforts to keep the economy on track by controlling the money supply are likely to have far more economic impact in an economy with imperfect competition than in a perfectly competitive world. That means that once economic fluctuations do occur, the government is better able to use monetary policy to do something about them.[13]

Another important factor that contributes to economic fluctuations is the imperfection of capital markets. The biggest, most modern industrial economies, such as those in the United States and Canada, Western Europe, and Japan, are highly dependent on centralized financial markets able to raise large sums of money quickly. As these markets become more closely interlinked, their imperfections, many of them having to do with inadequate information, incomplete markets, or poor institutional arrangements, have increasing power to affect the speed with which an economy grows and the seriousness of its cyclical downturns.

One important imperfection, for example, is the lack of complete markets in which companies can insure against all kinds of risks. There are ways of insuring against many kinds of risks. Insurance policies can protect against a customer who fails to pay his bill or an employee who steals company secrets, while futures and options contracts offer protection against future changes in exchange rates or in the prices of essential raw materials. But some risks are harder to protect against. Manufacturers, for example, must decide what their factories will produce long in advance of being able to sell those products. They make commitments to purchase equipment and material in the expectation of selling a certain amount of output for a certain price, and they have no way to protect themselves against changes in consumers' tastes or in the level of overall economic demand that might make their output less valuable and cause them to lose money.

If, for whatever reason, the economy's rate of growth suddenly slows, some companies' long-standing plans may look like losers rather than winners. Because those companies were not able to protect themselves fully against a fall in the demand for their products, the value of their stock will decline in response. That reduces the amount of equity they have to support their operations, limiting their ability to undertake new ventures. At the same time, other companies may benefit from the economic changes and the value of their stock may increase. But this sudden redistribution of wealth does not leave the economy unaffected. If the firms whose wealth has increased are unable to make use of the additional value of their stock as well as the firms whose wealth has diminished, the result will be a lower amount of investment in the economy as a whole, driving economic growth down.

At the same time, because of the lack of perfect information in the capital markets, this change in the circumstances of a large number of companies makes the detailed information that lenders have carefully collected about corporate plans and earnings prospects obsolete. Some companies will now be on a sounder footing than they were previously, but lending to others will entail greater risks than it previously did. Assessing the changed risk picture takes time. Some banks might temporarily pull back from lending altogether. Others might demand higher rates of interest or make loans only for shorter periods of time, at least until they better understand the new economic environment. If bank financing becomes harder to obtain because of this economic slowdown, the total amount of investment that occurs in the economy will fall, making the downturn deeper than it otherwise would be.[14]

The lack of perfect information in financial markets affects business cycles in another way as well. Lenders typically require borrowers to put up collateral, such as a mortgage on a piece of property or cash to cover a portion of the borrower's needs. This collateral protects the lender against his or her inability to understand fully the risks involved in the loan and also increases the borrower's incentive to repay on time. In general, the greater the collateral a borrower can bring to a project, the lower the lender will feel the risk to be and the less he or she will insist upon large downpayments, insurance premiums, credit investigations, audits, and other expenses that effectively raise the cost of borrowing. Once a recession begins, companies tend to become less solvent as their sales decline, particularly if this slowdown in sales is accompanied by a rise in the interest rates they must pay on their outstanding loans. Under those circumstances, lenders are likely to demand even greater collateral from potential customers. This, of course, makes it more expensive to borrow money. The higher cost of borrowing will cause companies to reduce the amount of investment they undertake even more than the incipient recession has already caused them to do, magnifying the effects of the downturn.[15]

Government policies that deal with these financial market imperfections may be important in keeping an economic slowdown from deteriorating into the total collapse of economic growth. One step the government can take is to impose strict requirements on the reporting of financial information by companies and financial institutions. As economic historians Barry Eichengreen and Richard Portes have observed, "Financial crises spread most quickly when information is least complete."[16] If lenders and investors are able to obtain accurate and up-to-date financial information about firms seeking loans and investments, they will be able to assess risks and expected returns more accurately, and the firms will not face unreasonable demands for collateral or insurance that drive up their borrowing costs unduly.

Another step involves assisting the development of better markets for risk and insurance. Many governments are skeptical of the desirability of futures markets, seeing them largely as places for speculation. But as we have seen, incomplete markets expose companies directly to risks that can magnify the effects of an economic downturn. The greater the variety of markets in which companies can hedge their bets and find others to share their risks, the easier it will be for them to bounce back from bad economic news.

Finally, of course, the government must regulate the structure of the financial markets so that a handful of defaults on loans or a sudden fall in stock prices does not cascade from firm to firm, leading to economic collapse. Financial markets are not just like other markets. They have a special role to play in the economy, and when they function poorly, many individuals whose money is not directly at stake will suffer if cutbacks in lending or investment occur. Measures such as bank deposit insurance, limits on the activities financial institutions may undertake, and rules to restrain speculation in stock and futures markets, all of which interfere with the operations of the free market and hence may reduce economic welfare in times of prosperity, are essential to keep slowdowns in economic growth from becoming deep troughs in the business cycle.

None of these policies will put an end to business cycles. The steady money growth rule recommended by the monetarists cannot stop them, and the activist fiscal and monetary policies popular in the 1960s and 1970s will not bring them under control. Indeed, there is something to be said for having cycles: they do act as a sort of cleansing agent in the economy, wiping out inefficient firms and unproductive jobs that managed to survive during periods of strong economic growth. That beneficial effect, however, does not mean that government should stand silently by and passively watch employment, investment, and consumption decline throughout the economy, as the rational expectations and real business cycle theories of the last few years would have it do. Carefully used, fiscal and monetary policies can stimulate an economy in depression or slow it when it overheats. And instruments of other sorts, such as those that discourage monopolistic behavior or improve the functioning of the financial markets, may help keep downturns from becoming as steep as they might otherwise be. The government may not be able to tame the business cycle altogether, but it does possess the ability to keep it from careening completely out of control.

11

The Lessons of the New Activist Economics

For the first time in over two decades, economists are able to offer a strong theoretical case for a government that acts to deal with economic problems rather than observing them passively from the sidelines. The inherited economic wisdom that shaped the conservative revolution, that the best government is that which governs least, now faces a strong challenge from these new understandings of how more government, rather than less government, can be the key to a better-running economy. But even as it defines a critical governmental role in improving economic welfare, the new activist economics offers little encouragement to those who would promote the policies of traditional political liberalism. A bigger welfare state, in which the government worries more about redistributing wealth than about increasing the size of the economic pie, is not what these new economic ideas prescribe. They suggest ways the government might help markets perform better when they fall short of perfection, not rationales for replacing markets altogether with government directives.

This theoretical understanding of the economic world is far more than 1960s Keynesianism warmed over. It draws heavily on the free market ideas of neoclassical economics, because the price system in a competitive market does fairly well—although far from perfectly—when it comes to guiding efficient economic choices. It rejects the empirically untenable assertions made by some earlier advocates of big government, who all too often justified their ideas by claiming that prices are "sticky," wages "rigid," and the level of investment "inadequate," without defensible explanations of those claims. And it focuses squarely on the issue of achieving the greatest possible efficiency and the highest possible output, rather than on a preoccupation with the distribution of income. Indeed, the new interventionism will disappoint many political liberals and social democrats because it rejects outright many of the economic precepts that have guided liberal political forces in North America and Europe for decades, precepts that rest more heavily on sympathy with individuals presumed to be disadvantaged than on an understanding of economic dynamics.

Most of all, the new activist economics is a skeptical economics. It teaches very clearly that the economic problems any society faces are far more complex than advocates of simplistic free market policies believe, but it also tells us that not all of those problems can be cured by government action. In trying to use the tools of government to improve economic well-being, the new activist economics is always cognizant that the optimal policies suggested by a theoretical analysis may look far different when translated into practice by a government of lawyers, politicians, and far-from-disinterested civil servants.

The most important lesson that emerges from the ideas discussed in this book is startling only because it so often has been forgotten by those offering economic prescriptions over the past two decades: good government is a complicated business.

The underlying goal of the conservative political movements of recent years, particularly in the United States, has been to reduce the discretion of those at the helm of governmental power. In areas of economic policy, this demand for less discretion has been translated into an insistence upon simple rules and formulas to regulate the government's actions. Research by economists has been critical to providing a scientific underpinning for such rules. On matters of monetary policy, for example, monetarists have insisted that central banks should adopt "monetary rules," steady paths for the growth of the money supply that should not be altered in response to current economic conditions. Many supply-siders have favored alternative rules tying monetary policy firmly to the prices of commodities or of gold, so that monetary growth would have to be increased or scaled back according to the dictates of an index not subject to government control. "Free trade is always best" is the simple rule to deal with foreign trade questions, and the statement that "financial markets are efficient" is offered as evidence against government regulations to control the functioning of the market. When antitrust issues arise, the question of whether the government should act against monopoly is easily settled by reference to the statement that whatever private companies choose to do is economically efficient, with competition, rather than regulation, forcing out inefficient practices; unless there is blatant price fixing, there is no need for government officials even to ponder enforcement actions. When it comes to unemployment, the rule advanced by believers in the workings of free markets is that eliminating obstacles to the adjustment of supply and demand in the labor market will allow wages to reach a level at which everyone who wants one can find a job.

In an age when bureaucracy is widely seen as a powerful enemy, these rules designed to curb bureaucratic discretion have strong appeal. But rules that automatically dictate how the government will act in a given situation are likely to lead to the greatest possible economic welfare only under a very special and improbable set of circumstances. Laissez-faire rules work just fine in hypothetical economies in which markets function perfectly and without friction. But they work poorly in real-world economies in which markets do not function in the textbook fashion. All of the popular rules for economic policy altogether lack the widespread applicability that their proponents claim. Under most economic conditions, there are carefully tailored government interventions that will make society better off than the automatic policy responses—or nonresponses—recommended by those who believe in small government before all else. The problem facing those who serve in government is to figure out just what those steps to improve public welfare might be, and to make sure that in the pull and tug of the political process they don't result in programs that end up making society poorer rather than richer.

In real life, people never have perfect information available before making business decisions, and they are unable to protect themselves fully against all of the diverse risks that arise in the course of business. In consequence, markets, be they labor markets, securities markets, product markets, or markets for foreign exchange, rarely operate in the perfectly frictionless way free market theories assume. The imperfections of the markets in which every-one participates on a daily basis, such as an employer's inability to monitor an individual worker's performance or an investor's diffi-culty comparing the risks involved in two alternative investments, may seem minor, even trivial. But these minor economic distortions can turn out to have major economic effects. They can cause thou-sands of workers to remain unemployed on a long-term basis and can make the entire economy much more sensitive to events that might trigger a slowdown in economic growth. If they exist on a large scale, they can result in a country's total output of goods and services remaining far below its potential unless the government in-tervenes to guide private economic decisions.

These flaws in the blackboard model of a picture-perfect econ-omy are rarely considered by those whose studies reveal no need for active government involvement in economic affairs. Nor do their studies normally postulate a messy world in which individ-uals, businesses, and countries carefully react to each others' moves in order to gain economic advantages instead of acting single-mindedly as if the other parties did not exist. But in this dynamic world of imperfect markets, the very concept of a government that is merely a passive observer of economic affairs is irrelevant, or even dangerous.

Take, for example, the frequent demand that governments ad-here to a rule of unrestrained free trade at all times. That rule is economically beneficial for everyone under the traditional assump-tion that each country that produces a given product is a small player in a highly competitive world market. But when a product is made by only a handful of firms around the world and its complex-ity makes it difficult for others to enter the business, those firms—and the governments of the countries in which they are located—may seek to use the lack of competition to drive prices up and profit at the expense of foreigners. Taking that step is usually dangerous, because if other governments retaliate everyone concerned may end up worse off. But if one government naively proclaims that it will adhere to a strict rule of free trade under all conditions, no matter how other governments act, others will be tempted to violate the norms of free trade and to seek to garner extra profits from their passive partner, perhaps making its citizens poorer as jobs and profits flow abroad. The prospect of retaliation will deter others from attempting to manipulate trade; a statement that there will never be retaliation can only encourage them to try manipulating trade.

Similarly, the argument that countries should allow market forces alone to determine the proper exchange rates of their currencies loses much of its force when any one important country fails to keep its end of the bargain. If other governments passively allow it to do what it wants with its own currency by steadfastly refusing to intervene on behalf of theirs under any circumstances, the country that breaks the rules will arrange its economic policies so as to achieve its own goals—a large trade surplus, for example, or the development of domestic manufacturing to supplant imported goods—at the expense of its trading partners. A declaration on the part of any nation that it will never attempt to control its exchange rate is an invitation to others to undertake such efforts to its disadvantage.

These strategic issues also enter into play when it comes to enforcing laws designed to maintain competition in the economy. Companies, after all, are not motivated solely by short-term economic considerations and a desire to increase their operating efficiency. Many actions and policies that corporations claim to have adopted for reasons of efficiency are in reality designed to reduce competition and thereby generate higher profits in the long run. A government antitrust policy that assumes companies seek solely to maximize profits each quarter and ignores these strategic dimensions of corporate behavior may fail to understand the anticompetitive potential of individual companies' actions, actions that may superficially appear to have reasonable business justifications but that may end up reducing the nation's economic well-being.

Remaining aloof from economic affairs means that a government is unable to deal with others' attempts to manipulate economic outcomes and with flaws in the markets that keep competition from working as well as it might. Only if government is involved in dealing with such problems can a nation's economy achieve its potential. The important question is not whether activist government is desirable but rather how to do it best.

But the suggestions offered by the new activist economics about how to do it best will not be appealing to many proponents of a large and powerful government. Traditionally, advocates of interventionist government have focused on "demand management," the far-ranging set of economic policies that directly affect the growth of the gross national product. The great economic debates of our time have concerned whether monetary and fiscal policies can be used in a deliberate way to raise consumers' demand for goods and services and businesses' demand for new plants, offices, and equipment, thus permanently increasing a country's total economic output. Where most Keynesians have long answered that question with a resounding "yes," the new generation of macroeconomic scholars offers a far less confident "yes, but . . ."

To be sure, some of the fundamental ideas supporting the emphasis on using the government's powers in order to control economic demand do hold true. For example, monetary policy has an important effect in controlling how fast the economy can grow. The old hard-money argument that in the long run monetary policy affects only the inflation rate, not the number of jobs or the amount of output, which in recent times has been put into scientific language by the monetarists, has been debunked by a growing number of studies showing that this impotence is the case only under one special circumstance, namely when all prices in the economy respond instantaneously to changes in demand. If, on the other hand, prices are even the slightest bit rigid, whether through imperfect competition, a poor flow of information, the cost of posting new prices, behavior that falls slightly short of "rationality," or some other factor, monetary policy has very real effects on employment and production.

But while reaffirming the importance of active control of the money supply, the new activist theories show that monetary policy is far more complicated than generally believed. Even the most basic lesson of the economics textbooks—faster money growth means higher output (at least in the short run) while slower money growth means economic contraction—does not necessarily hold true. One of the surprising and controversial new propositions about monetary policy is that the precise effects of money supply changes depend very much on how close prices are to the levels they would have in a perfectly competitive economy. If prices are just slightly out of line now—if prices are only slightly sticky and adjust to changed conditions without extremely long delays—companies might not bother to change them when the money supply increases slightly tomorrow. That small increase in the amount of money in the economy will then lead to a big jump in economic output. If, in contrast, prices are so sticky that they are far below the competitive level because most businesses have not raised them in response to money supply changes for months or years, a tiny increase in money supply growth now might be enough to trigger a round of sharp price hikes, causing the economy to *contract* rather than to expand![1] This, of course, runs directly contrary to the standard assumptions about how monetary policy works.

In addition, the effects of monetary policy depend critically upon how it alters international capital flows. Changes in the money supply, after all, are supposed to have their major economic impact by changing interest rates: faster money growth means more money is in circulation, so the cost of borrowing should fall. But those lower interest rates will also cause the exchange rate to fall as investors move their money to other countries. If capital is so sensitive to changes in the return it can earn that a given money supply increase causes a large amount of capital to move abroad, the funds available for domestic borrowing may shrink so far that domestic interest rates go back up.

This presents a confusing picture for central bankers. The monetary tools at their disposal clearly have real effects on the economy, changing the total amount of output and the relative amounts of the various goods and services that are produced. But exactly how any change in monetary policy will alter the economy's performance is impossible to foresee. The only feasible policy is a most inelegant one, successive approximation: the monetary authorities must make small changes in policy, see what happens to the economy, and then adjust course accordingly.

The new activist theories suggest that government fiscal policies too have direct and lasting effects on the level of aggregate demand. Many economists in recent years have argued otherwise, contending that when a change in the level of government spending or taxation changes the amount of economic demand, individuals and businesses quickly adjust their prices upward or downward in the same proportion, leaving inflation-adjusted output unchanged. Their doubts about the standard explanations of how fiscal policy works—spending increases and tax cuts are expansionary, spending cuts and tax increases cause the economy to contract—are well founded, but the assertion that fiscal policies are powerless to affect the economy's performance is not.

The original basis for using fiscal policy to regulate economic performance was Keynes's contention that fiscal policy has a "multiplier" effect, with one additional dollar or pound of government spending resulting in several times that much increase in the economy's output. Opponents of activist fiscal policy contend, in essence, that the multiplier is one—each dollar of expenditures by the government increases total economic output by only one dollar—and that it may even be less than one if the dollar the government spends could have been used more efficiently by those who paid it in taxes. Advocates of fiscal activism have traditionally responded that the multiplier is positive and large, with each dollar of spending rebounding through the economy several times and thus powerfully stimulating demand.

Neither of these propositions appears to be completely correct. Economic theory offers no particular reason why the effects of fiscal policy should necessarily be the same at every moment: fiscal stimulus might do much to increase investment spending at a time when investment spending is low but have negligible impact when investment spending is already high. The assertion that fiscal policy can have no long-standing economic effects under any circumstances is too extreme. But even most advocates of activist fiscal policies would now admit that spending and taxation are extremely crude tools for controlling the overall level of demand in the economy. How much a dollar of government spending will increase investment or consumption depends very much upon what that dollar buys; not all spending is equally stimulative. And under some circumstances, it turns out, fiscal policies can have the opposite effects from those in the textbook models, with tax cuts causing the economy to *contract* rather than to expand.[2] To confuse matters further, in an economy open to world trade and capital flows, a large budget deficit that would normally be considered highly expansionary may necessitate foreign borrowing, which drives up the exchange rate, encouraging imports while reducing exports and thus counteracting its own stimulative effects. These complexities make it almost impossible to calculate a single "fiscal multiplier" by which the effects of possible changes in taxation or spending can easily be measured. The fiscal policy tool has real economic power, but it is a difficult tool to control.

In terms of shaping government intervention in economic affairs, then, the new activist economics departs sharply from the conventional understandings. It completely rejects the findings of monetarist and rational expectationist theories that find no possibility for active government policies to improve economic welfare. But with equal firmness, it disavows the common perception that by tinkering with two big levers labeled "monetary policy" and "fiscal policy" a nation's political and economic leaders can steer the economy so as to make everyone as well off as possible. Those levers can be used in a crude way to push the economy in the direction of faster or slower growth, but they will not be adequate to deal with the problems of unemployment, trade flows, and capital accumulation that confront governments in the modern world. For those purposes, policymakers must pay close attention to microeconomics.

Microeconomics—the study of particular markets within the economy—has until recent years been a stepchild within the economics profession. The great economic thinkers, the ones whose names are constantly in the press and whose views are eagerly sought by political leaders, are known for their comments on the major macroeconomic issues: How big should the budget be? How much should taxes be cut? Is monetary policy too restrictive? Analysis of the microeconomic details of government policy has generally been a far less prestigious undertaking than elucidation of the Big Picture.

Although microeconomics underwent a revival starting in the 1970s, led by George Stigler and others at the University of Chicago who reconsidered the nature of competition within individual industries, the scholars involved were all firm believers in the workings of the free market. Their analysis was designed to show how markets from medical care to passenger aviation could work just fine without government regulation and could achieve the greatest degree of wealth for the entire economy in the process. Economists who worried about such things as imperfect markets remained, by

and large, aloof from these microeconomic debates. Their understanding of the world offered no clear linkage between the microeconomic functioning of thousands of individual markets and the
macroeconomy those markets compose. In fact, most of the theories
calling for active government management of economic affairs
were not grounded in a microeconomic understanding of how individual markets work, and many economists simply ignored such
questions.

The new activist economics, by contrast, places great weight on
microeconomic questions. In this, it shares the fundamental belief
of free market economists that an entire national economy cannot
function smoothly unless the smaller product and service markets
within it are also working well. One of its major contributions is to
show how seemingly minor shortcomings in individual markets
within the economy can lead to major economic problems affecting
the economy as a whole. This way of looking at the economy from
the bottom up constitutes a distinct departure from the past emphasis of Keynesian and social democratic thinkers on the overall
picture rather than on its component parts. It brings with it a very
different perspective on what the government can do to help the
economy achieve its full potential. While monetary and fiscal policies are not unimportant, the devil is in the details.

In years past, the litmus test of whether a politician qualified as
"liberal" or "leftist" was often his or her willingness to stimulate
the economy to create jobs. But one of the contentions of the new
activist teaching is that traditional economic stimulus, whether of
the fiscal or monetary variety, will have only limited success in the
battle against unemployment. Faster growth will put some people
back to work, but it won't resolve the problems of risk and poor
information that cause individual employers to pay higher wages
than they need to attract workers, and to hire fewer workers as a
result. Addressing those microeconomic issues is far tougher than
simply increasing government spending. It may require changes in
the details of dozens of laws governing employment relationships,
concerning such matters as potential employers' information about
the workers they are contemplating hiring and their ability to protect against the risk of poor employee performance. Certain kinds
of government employment subsidies or risk-sharing programs may

be useful too, but they must be carefully designed to deal with specific problems that inhibit the smooth functioning of the labor market. Because the reasons employers choose not to hire as many workers as they might vary widely, no single nationwide approach is likely to be adequate. A variety of efforts, each designed to deal with a specific labor market problem, will be required.

A similar attention to detail is needed to shape effective policies regarding trade. A country that tries to protect its own industries with tariffs and trade barriers usually causes itself economic harm in the process. But if a foreign country is using subsidies, barriers, and other techniques to help one of its own companies keep competitors from gaining a foothold in an emerging industry, other nations must be prepared to respond lest the foreigners obtain the power to extract excessive profits at the expense of their trading partners. Completely free trade may not the best course. But neither crude macroeconomic responses, such as exchange rate manipulation, nor the measures routinely demanded by companies claiming they have been injured by imports, such as tariffs or quotas, are likely to make the importing country better off. The best policy will likely be a collection of measures closely tailored to the specific situation at hand, designed as carefully as possible to maintain a high degree of competition without leading to the inefficiencies that can easily arise when a producer finds it too easy fall back on government support.

These cautious approaches may be anathema to believers in leaving economic matters to the free market, but they will be just as uncomfortable for most fans of the welfare state. Massive government spending programs—programs that appear to be coming back into political vogue in industrial countries after being suppressed by the conservative political waves of the early 1980s—have little in common with the carefully designed initiatives the new activist economics recommends. And the new activism does not share the utopian belief that a big dose of government can make the economy run with full employment indefinitely. Government programs, these new understandings suggest, must be designed with careful attention to such details as their effects on individual incentives to work and invest, on the allocation of economic risk, and on the flow of information within the economy. The welfare state programs of the 1960s and 1970s rarely kept such considerations in mind.

Activist government of the sort this analysis suggests is not without its risks. Political needs rather than considerations of the greater good may threaten to drive many of the government's actions. And the civil servants who must make the hard decisions about which specific actions should be undertaken can hardly be considered disinterested, totally objective observers; concerns about their own careers and their organizations' self-interest are bound to play a role. In individual cases, whether by accident or design, the choices they make may prove wrong, leaving economic damage in their wake. But despite these dangers, there is no real alternative to bureaucratic discretion. Clear and simple rules to tell the bureaucrats what to do, or the even simpler libertarian contention that they should do nothing at all, are ill-suited to a world of imperfect markets, strategic behavior, and constantly changing economic relationships.

At the dawn of the 1980s, it was fashionable to proclaim the dissolution of economic science. Growing differences of opinion over the way the economy works led to what was widely perceived as the failure of macroeconomics. Monetarists and rational expectationists had apparently relegated the long-established Keynesian wisdom to the status of a historical curiosity, but their own models of an economy with perfect markets and perfectly rational individuals bore little resemblance to the world they were seeking to illuminate. As sociologist Irving Kristol complained, "The existence of a 'crisis in economic theory' is attested to by the fact that this body of *undisputed* theory is shrinking before our very eyes, not growing. More and more of the intellectual energy of economists, these days, goes into the *dis*establishment of what our university textbooks still proclaim with serene confidence. Almost everything—almost every concept, every theorem, every methodology—in economics today has become fair game for controversy."[3]

The new activist economics of the 1980s represents a movement that may bring together, rather than further tear apart, the major trends in economic thought. That certainly does not mean that economists will henceforth agree on how governments and central banks ought to make economic policy. But by combining the traditional Keynesian understanding of an economically imperfect world with the rigorous analytical methods introduced by free market theorists, while giving particular emphasis to the importance of people's economic expectations in shaping the course of events, these new ideas suggest that there are many economic issues on which economists of all schools of thought can find common ground.

They will not, to be sure, make theory less disputed. The fancy new mathematical tools that have become part and parcel of economics make disagreement all too easy: as the language of the profession has changed from words to simple equations to complex mathematical and statistical statements of economic ideas, any graduate student can posit a different set of assumptions and reach conclusions radically different from those of prior researchers. Nonetheless, this new economic framework, still very much under construction, suggests principles for analyzing economic issues that transcend the traditional philosophical divisions within the economics profession. At the same time, it offers important guidance for the management of economic policy in an imperfect world, guidance that seems to be in line with the developing political currents of the late twentieth century.

Notes

Introduction

1. See, for example, Robert Kuttner, "The Poverty of Economics," *The Atlantic* 255:2 (Feb. 1985):74.
2. William G. Dewald, Jerry G. Thursby, and Richard G. Anderson, "Replication in Empirical Economics," *American Economic Review* 76:4 (Sept. 1986):587.

Chapter 1
The Rise of the Free Marketeers

1. Marc Levinson, "Comeback for Keynes?" *Dun's Business Month* 127:1 (Jan. 1986):39.
2. James M. Buchanan, "Quest for a Tempered Utopia," *Wall Street Journal*, Nov. 14, 1986, p. 30.
3. Susan Lee, "The Un-managed Economy," *Forbes* 134:12 (Dec. 17, 1984):147.
4. As examples of this genre, see Robert J. Genetski, *Taking the Voodoo Out of Economics* (Lake Bluff, Ill.: Regnery Gateway, 1986); Stuart M. Butler, *Privatizing Federal Spending* (New York: Universe Books, 1985); Gordon Jackson, "All Supply-Siders Now?" *Policy Review* no. 41 (Summer 1987); and Gordon Tullock, *Economics of Income Redistribution* (Boston, The Hague, and London: Kluwer Nijhoff, 1983).
5. Carolyn Lochhead, "A Lesson in Economic Life Is Turning the Keynesian Tide," *Insight* 3:23 (June 8, 1987):38–40.
6. John Maynard Keynes, *The General Theory of Employment, Interest, and Money* (New York: Harcourt Brace Jovanovich, 1964), 320.
7. Ibid., 162.
8. Ibid., 3.
9. See the comments of James Tobin in Arjo Klamer, *Conversations with Economists* (Totowa, N.J.: Rowman & Allenheld, 1984), 103.

10. Walter W. Heller, *New Dimensions of Political Economy* (Cambridge: Harvard University Press, 1966), 116.
11. Paul A. Samuelson, *Economics*, 8th ed. (New York: McGraw-Hill, 1970), 250.
12. Herbert Stein, *Presidential Economics* (New York: Simon and Schuster, 1984), 135.
13. George Stigler, "Nobel Lecture: The Process and Progress of Economics," *Journal of Political Economy* 91:3 (Aug. 1983):529–45; Michael R. Darby and James R. Lothian, "Economic Events and Keynesian Ideas: The 1930s and the 1970s," in *Keynes's General Theory, Fifty Years On*, ed. John Burton (London: Institute of Economic Affairs, 1986).
14. Milton Friedman, "The Role of Monetary Policy," *American Economic Review* 58:1 (March 1968):1–17.
15. For a technical explanation of rational expectations theory, see R.E. Lucas, Jr., "Expectations and the Neutrality of Money," *Journal of Economic Theory* 4:1 (1972):103–24; and T.J. Sargent and N. Wallace, "Rational Expectations and Optimal Monetary Instrument and the Optimal Money Supply Rule," *Journal of Political Economy* 83:2 (May 1983):241–54. For a nontechnical version, see Bennett T. McCallum, "The Significance of Rational Expectations Theory," *Challenge* 22:6 (Jan.–Feb. 1980):37–43.
16. Klamer, *Conversations*, 52.
17. See the symposium, "The Contribution of Keynes After 50 Years," in *American Economic Review* 77:2 (May 1987):125–42; and George Akerlof and Janet Yellen, "Can Small Deviations from Rationality Make Significant Differences to Economic Equilibria?" *American Economic Review* 75:4 (Sept. 1985):708–20.
18. Milton Friedman, *Capitalism and Freedom* (Chicago: University of Chicago Press, 1962).
19. David Kelley, "Marketplace of Ideas," *Barron's*, Jan. 14, 1980, p. 9.

Chapter 2
The Reagan Experiment

1. "Why Supply-Side Economics Is Suddenly Popular," *Business Week*, Sept. 17, 1979, p. 116.
2. For a clear economic statement of the supply-side approach, see Michael K. Evans, "The Bankruptcy of Keynesian Econometric Models," *Challenge* 22:6 (Jan.–Feb. 1980):13. The best attempt at a theoretical grounding is to be found in David G. Raboy, ed., *Essays in Supply Side Economics* (Washington:

Institute for Research in the Economics of Taxation/The Heritage Foundation, 1982). For a cogent critique, see Stephen Rousseas, "Return of the Economic Royalists," *Challenge* 24:6 (Jan.–Feb. 1982):36.

3. George Gilder, *Wealth and Poverty* (New York: Basic Books, 1981), 195.

4. "A Guide to Understanding the Supply-Siders," *Business Week*, Dec. 22, 1980, p. 76.

5. *Economic Report of the President 1983* (Washington, D.C.: U.S. Government Printing Office, 1983), 25.

6. Irving Kristol, "Rationalism in Economics," in *The Crisis in Economic Theory*, ed. Daniel Bell and Irving Kristol (New York: Basic Books, 1981), 202.

7. Gilder, *Wealth and Poverty*, 261.

8. Joke cited by Alan Greenspan in comments to the annual meeting of the National Association of Business Economists, Boston, Mass., Sept. 18, 1986.

9. Weekly Compilation of Presidential Documents, Feb. 23, 1981, 17:8, p. 141.

10. *Economic Report of the President 1982* (Washington, D.C.: U.S. Government Printing Office, 1982), chap. 2, 3.

11. Murray Weidenbaum, *Today's Challenges to Economic Freedom*, Contemporary Issues Series, no. 23 (St. Louis: Center for the Study of American Business, 1987).

12. *Economic Report of the President 1982*, 23.

13. "A Program for Economic Recovery," The White House, Feb. 18, 1981, pp. 24–25.

14. Thomas J. Sargent and Neil Wallace, "Some Unpleasant Monetarist Arithmetic," *Federal Reserve Bank of Minneapolis Quarterly Review* 5:4 (Fall 1981):1–7.

15. Testimony of Treasury Secretary Donald T. Regan before the Joint Economic Committee, Jan. 27, 1982; President's Proposal for Tax Reduction, Feb. 18, 1981, p. 6.

16. "A Program for Economic Recovery," "Budget Reform Package," p. 12.

17. Heritage Foundation, *Agenda for Progress* (Washington, D.C.: Heritage Foundation, 1981).

18. *Economic Report of the President 1982*, 43, 134–65.

19. Barry P. Bosworth, *Taxes and the Investment Recovery*, Brookings Papers on Economic Activity, no. 1 (Washington, D.C.: Brookings Institution, 1985), 1; Lawrence B. Lindsey, *Taxpayer Behavior and the Distribution of the 1982 Tax Cut*, NBER Working Paper no. 1760 (Cambridge, Mass.: National Bureau of Economic Research, 1985).

20. William H. Branson, *The Limits of Monetary Coordination as Exchange Rate Policy*, Brookings Papers on Economic Activity, no. 1 (Washington, D.C.: The Brookings Institution, 1986), 175; William H. Branson and James P. Love, *Dollar Appreciation and Manufacturing Employment and Output*, NBER Working Paper no. 1972 (Cambridge, Mass.: National Bureau of Economic Research, 1986); Martin Feldstein, *The Budget Deficit and the Dollar*, NBER Working Paper no. 1898 (Cambridge, Mass.: National Bureau of Economic Research, 1986).

21. Marc Levinson, "Small Business: Myth and Reality," *Dun's Business Month* 126:3 (Sept. 1985):30.
22. See Regan's testimony before the Joint Economic Committee, Jan. 26, 1984; Sprinkel's remarks to Financial Executives Institute, New York, Dec. 7, 1983; and Sprinkel's testimony before the Senate Committee on Banking, Housing, and Urban Affairs, Feb. 9, 1984.
23. Marc Levinson, "Economic Policy: The Old Tools Won't Work," *Dun's Business Month* 129:1 (Jan. 1987):30.
24. "The Problem of Monetarism," Dec. 4, 1985, p. 30.
25. Gene Koretz, "A Tighter Job Market Puts Inflation Closer to Its Flash Point," *Business Week*, March 28, 1988, p. 20.

Chapter 3
Activist Economics Comes Back

1. Benjamin M. Friedman, "Recent Perspectives in and on Macroeconomics," in *Issues in Contemporary Macroeconomics and Distribution*, ed. George R. Feiwel (London: Macmillan, 1985), 281.
2. N. Gregory Mankiw, "Issues in Keynesian Macroeconomics: A Review Essay," *Journal of Monetary Economics* 18:2 (1986):217–23.
3. Perhaps the most notable exception is the work of Thomas E. Weisskopf, Samuel Bowles, and David M. Gordon, such as *Hearts and Minds: A Social Model of U.S. Productivity Growth*, Brookings Papers in Economic Activity no. 2 (Washington, D.C.: Brookings Institution, 1983):381–439; and *Beyond the Wasteland* (New York: Anchor-Doubleday, 1983).
4. A discussion of this problem may be found in Joseph Bower, *When Markets Quake* (Cambridge, Mass.: Harvard Business School Press, 1986).
5. Irwin Lipnowski and Shlomo Maital, "Hanging Together or Separately: A Game-Theoretic Approach to Macroeconomic Conflict," in *Macroeconomic Conflict and Social Institutions*, ed. Shlomo Maital and Irwin Lipnowski (Cambridge, Mass: Ballinger, 1985), 39–94.
6. This classic problem of market failure was first outlined in George Akerlof, "The Market for Lemons: Qualitative Uncertainty and the Market Mechanism," *Quarterly Journal of Economics* 84:2 (April 1970):288–300.
7. Joseph E. Stiglitz and Andrew Weiss, "Macro-economic Equilibrium and Credit Rationing," (Bell Communications Research, 1986, mimeo).
8. See the discussion in Tibor Scitovsky, *The Joyless Economy* (New York: Oxford University Press, 1976).

Chapter 4
Understanding Unemployment

1. James W. Dean, "The Dissolution of the Keynesian Consensus," in *The Crisis in Economic Theory*, ed. Daniel Bell and Irving Kristol (New York: Basic Books, 1981), 34.
2. Marc Levinson, "The New Interventionist Economists," *The New Leader* 59:3 (Feb. 10, 1986):7.
3. Milton Friedman, "The Role of Monetary Policy," *American Economic Review* 58:1 (March 1968):1–17.
4. John Maynard Keynes, *The General Theory of Employment, Interest, and Money* (New York: Harcourt Brace Jovanovich, 1964), chap. 19.
5. A.W. Phillips, "The Relation between Unemployment and the Rate of Change of Money Wage Rates in the United Kingdom, 1861–1957," *Economica* 25:4 (Nov. 1958):283–99.
6. Robert E. Lucas, Jr., "Unemployment Policy," *American Economic Review* 68:2 (May 1978):353–56.
7. J. Peter Neary and Joseph E. Stiglitz, "Toward a Reconstruction of Keynesian Economics: Expectations and Constrained Equilibria," *Quarterly Journal of Economics* 99:2 (May 1984):199–228.
8. Robert E. Lucas, Jr., and Leonard A. Rapping, "Price Expectations and the Phillips Curve," *American Economic Review* 59:3 (June 1969):342–50.
9. Joseph E. Stiglitz, "Theories of Wage Rigidity," in *Keynes' Economic Legacy: Contemporary Economic Theories*, ed. James L. Butkiewicz, Kenneth J. Koford, and Jeffrey B. Miller (New York: Praeger, 1986), 153–206; Lawrence F. Katz, "Efficiency Wage Theories: A Partial Evaluation," in *NBER Macroeconomics Annual 1986*, ed. Stanley Fischer (Cambridge, Mass.: MIT Press, 1986), 235–76.
10. Carl Shapiro and Joseph E. Stiglitz, "Equilibrium Unemployment as a Worker Discipline Device," *American Economic Review* 74:3 (June 1984):433–44. For elaborations, see William T. Dickens, Lawrence Katz, and Kevin Lang, *Are Efficiency Wages Efficient?* NBER Working Paper no. 1935 (Cambridge, Mass.: National Bureau of Economic Research, 1986); George A. Akerlof and Lawrence F. Katz, *Do Deferred Wages Dominate Involuntary Unemployment as a Worker Discipline Device?* NBER Working Paper no. 2025 (Cambridge, Mass.: National Bureau of Economic Research, 1986); and Ekkehart Schlicht, "Dismissal vs. Fines as a Discipline Device"(manuscript, 1985).
11. Andrew Weiss, "Job Queues and Layoffs in Labor Markets with Flexible Wages," *Journal of Political Economy* 88:3 (May 1980):526–38.
12. George Akerlof, "Gift Exchange and Efficiency Wage Theory: Four Views," *American Economic Review, Papers and Proceedings* 74:2 (May 1984): 79–83.

13. Alan B. Krueger and Lawrence H. Summers, "Reflections on the Inter-Industry Wage Structure," in *Unemployment and the Structure of Labor Markets*, ed. K. Lang and J. Leonard (New York: Basil Blackwell, 1987) and "Efficiency Wages and the Inter-Industry Wage Structure," *Econometrica* 56:1 (March 1988):259–94.

14. Daniel Kahneman, Jack L. Knetsch, and Richard Thaler, "Fairness as a Constraint on Profit Seeking: Entitlements in the Market," *American Economic Review* 76:4 (Sept. 1986):728–41.

15. William T. Dickens and Lawrence F. Katz, *Inter-Industry Wage Differences and Theories of Wage Determination*, NBER Working Paper no. 2271 (Cambridge, Mass.: National Bureau of Economic Research, 1987).

16. Jeremy I. Bulow and Lawrence H. Summers, "A Theory of Dual Labor Markets with Application to Industrial Policy, Discrimination and Keynesian Unemployment," *Journal of Labor Economics* 4:3, pt. 1 (July 1986):376–414.

17. See the discussion in Richard Arnott, Arthur Hosios, and Joseph Stiglitz, *Implicit Contracts, Labor Mobility and Unemployment*, NBER Working Paper no. 2316 (Cambridge, Mass.: National Bureau of Economic Research, 1987).

Chapter 5
We're All Monetarists Now

1. Milton Friedman, *A Program for Monetary Stability* (New York: Fordham University Press, 1960); Milton Friedman and Anna J. Schwartz, *A Monetary History of the United States* (Princeton: Princeton University Press, 1963).

2. Milton Friedman, "The Role of Monetary Policy," *American Economic Review* 58:1 (March 1968):1–17.

3. For surveys of monetarist and rational expectationist views of monetary policy in nontechnical language, see James Tobin, "Monetarism: An Ebbing Tide?" *The Economist*, April 27, 1985, pp. 23–25, and James W. Dean, "The Rise and Fall of Neomonetarism," *Financial Analysts Journal* 41:5 (Sept.–Oct. 1985):72–77.

4. John Huizinga and Frederic S. Mishkin, *Monetary Policy Regime Shifts and the Unusual Behavior of Real Interest Rates*, Carnegie-Rochester Conference Series on Public Policy, vol. 24 (Amsterdam: North Holland, 1986), 231–74.

5. Allan Meltzer, interview with the author, Pittsburgh, Pa., June 19, 1986.

6. William Poole, "Monetary Policy Lessons of Recent Inflation and Disinflation," *Journal of Economic Perspectives* 2:3 (Summer 1988).

7. Herbert Stein, *Presidential Economics* (New York: Simon and Schuster, 1984), 330.

8. For an argument in support of such a policy, see Robert J. Barro, "Recent

Developments in the Theory of Rules versus Discretion," *Economic Journal*, supplement (1985):23–37.

9. Marc Levinson, "New Linchpin for the Dollar," *Business Month* 129:6 (June 1987):24–25.

10. N. Gregory Mankiw, "Small Menu Costs and Large Business Cycles: A Macroeconomic Model of Monopoly," *Quarterly Journal of Economics* 100:2 (May 1985):529–39; Olivier Blanchard and Nobuhiro Kiyotaki, "Monopolistic Competition and the Effects of Aggregate Demand," *American Economic Review* 77:4 (Sept. 1987):647–66.

11. Bruce Greenwald and Joseph E. Stiglitz, *Money, Imperfect Information and Economic Fluctuations*, NBER Working Paper no. 2188 (Cambridge, Mass.: National Bureau of Economic Research, 1987); Alan S. Blinder and Joseph E. Stiglitz, "Money, Credit Constraints, and Economic Activity," *American Economic Review* 72:2 (May 1983):297–302.

12. George A. Akerlof and Janet L. Yellen, "A Near-Rational Model of the Business Cycle, with Wage and Price Inertia," *Quarterly Journal of Economics* 100, supplement (1985): 823–38.

Chapter 6
Inefficient Markets

1. Charles P. Kindleberger, *Manias, Panics, and Crashes* (New York: Basic Books, 1978).

2. John Maynard Keynes, *The General Theory of Employment, Interest and Money* (New York: Harcourt Brace Jovanovich, 1964), 159.

3. Michael C. Jensen and Richard S. Ruback, "The Market for Corporate Control," *Journal of Finance* 11:1–4 (April 1983):5–50.

4. Robert A. Taggart, Jr., "The Growth of the 'Junk' Bond Market and Its Role in Financing Takeovers," in *Mergers and Acquisitions*, ed. Alan J. Auerbach (Chicago: University of Chicago Press, 1987).

5. Alison Leigh Cowan, "Awash in Dow Ebb and Flow," *New York Times*, May 14, 1987, p. D1.

6. Barbara Donnelly, "Investors' Overreactions May Yield Opportunities in the Stock Market," *Wall Street Journal*, Jan. 7, 1988, p. 21; James M. Poterba and Lawrence H. Summers, *Mean Reversion in Stock Prices: Evidence and Implications*, Harvard Institute of Economic Research Discussion Paper no. 1349 (Cambridge, Mass.: Harvard University, 1987).

7. Sanford J. Grossman and Joseph E. Stiglitz, "On the Impossibility of Informationally Efficient Markets," *American Economic Review* 70:3 (June 1980):393–408.

8. For surveys of efficient market theory, see Eugene F. Fama, "Efficient Capital Markets: A Review of Theory and Empirical Work," *Journal of Finance* 25:2 (May 1970):383–417; and Margaret Bray, "Rational Expectations, Information and Asset Markets: An Introduction," *Oxford Economic Papers* 37:2 (1985):161–95.

9. Eugene H. Hawkins, Stanley C. Chamberlin, and Wayne E. Daniel, "Earnings Expectations and Security Prices," *Financial Analysts Journal* 40:5 (Sept.–Oct. 1984):24–38; Richard S. Bower and Dorothy H. Bower, "The Salomon Brothers Electric Utility Model: Another Challenge to Market Efficiency," *Financial Analysts Journal* 40:5 (Sept.–Oct. 1984), pp. 57–67.

10. N. Gregory Mankiw and Lawrence H. Summers, *Do Long-Term Interest Rates Overreact to Short-Term Interest Rates?* Brookings Papers on Economic Activity, no. 1 (Washington, D.C.: Brookings Institution, 1984), 223–42.

11. Arlene Hershman, "You Might Beat the Market Because . . . " *Dun's Business Month* 124:4 (Oct. 1984):78–83.

12. Robert J. Shiller, *Stock Prices and Social Dynamics*, Brookings Papers on Economic Activity, no. 2 (Washington, D.C.: Brookings Institution, 1984), 457–98.

13. John Pound and Robert J. Shiller, *Speculative Behavior of Institutional Investors*, NBER Working Paper no. 1964 (Cambridge, Mass.: National Bureau of Economic Research, 1986).

14. Charles R. Plott, "Laboratory Experiments in Economics: The Implications of Posted Price Institutions," *Science* 232:5 (May 1986).

15. Vernon L. Smith, "Experimental Methods in the Political Economy of Exchange," *Science* 234:4773 (Oct. 10, 1986):167–73.

16. Charles R. Plott, "Rational Choice in Experimental Markets," *Journal of Business* 59:4, pt. 2 (1986):S301-27.

17. Marc Levinson, "Using Science to Bid for Business," *Business Month* 129:4 (April 1987):50–51.

18. Bruce Greenwald, Joseph E. Stiglitz, and Andrew Weiss, "Informational Imperfections in the Capital Markets and Macro-Economic Fluctuations," *American Economic Review* 74:2 (May 1984):194–200.

19. N. Gregory Mankiw, "The Allocation of Credit and Financial Collapse," *Quarterly Journal of Economics* 101:3 (Aug. 1986):455–70.

Chapter 7
The Mess in the Currency Markets

1. Gottfried Haberler, "The Choice of Exchange Rates After the War," *American Economic Review* 35:3 (June 1945):308–18.

2. Raymond F. Mikesell, *Foreign Exchange in the Postwar World* (New York: Twentieth Century Fund, 1954), 490.
3. William Fellner, "On Limited Exchange Rate Flexibility," in *Maintaining and Restoring Balance in International Payments*, ed. William Fellner et al. (Princeton: Princeton University Press, 1966), 490.
4. Milton Friedman, "The Case for Flexible Exchange Rates," in *Essays in Positive Economics*, ed. Milton Friedman (Chicago: University of Chicago Press, 1953), 157–203.
5. Gottfried Haberler and Thomas D. Willett, *U.S. Balance-of-Payments Policies and International Monetary Reform: A Critical Analysis* (Washington, D.C.: American Enterprise Institute, 1968).
6. See especially Milton Friedman and Robert V. Roosa, *The Balance of Payments: Free versus Fixed Exchange Rates* (Washington, D.C.: American Enterprise Institute, 1967), 10–15.
7. Ibid., 20.
8. Thomas D. Willett, *Floating Exchange Rates and International Monetary Reform* (Washington, D.C.: American Enterprise Institute, 1977), chap. 2.
9. John Williamson, *The Exchange Rate System*, 2d ed. (Washington, D.C.: Institute for International Economics, 1985); John Y. Campbell and Richard H. Clarida, "The Dollar and Real Interest Rates," in *Carnegie-Rochester Conference Series on Public Policy* (Amsterdam: North Holland, 1987).
10. Jeffrey A. Frankel and Kenneth A. Froot, *The Dollar as an Irrational Speculative Bubble: A Tale of Fundamentalists and Chartists*, Wallenberg Papers in International Finance, vol. 1, no. 1 (Washington: International Law Institute, 1986), 27–55.
11. Paul R. Krugman, "Exchange Rate Instability" (Robbins Lectures), (mimeo.), Cambridge, Mass.: Massachusetts Institute of Technology, 1988.
12. Jeffrey A. Frankel, *Six Possible Meanings of "Overvaluation": The 1981–85 Dollar*, Essays in International Finance no. 159 (Princeton: Princeton University International Finance Section, 1987).
13. John H. Makin, "Coordination of Fiscal Policies under Flexible Exchange Rates," in *U.S. Fiscal Policy: Its Effects at Home and Abroad*, ed. John H. Makin (Washington: American Enterprise Institute, 1986). Also see the insightful comments of Otmar Emminger, former president of the German central bank, in *The Dollar's Borrowed Strength* (New York: Group of Thirty, 1985).
14. Jacob A. Frenkel, "International Interdependence and the Constraints on Macroeconomic Policies," in *How Open Is the U.S. Economy*, ed. R.W. Hafer (Lexington, Mass.: Lexington Books, 1986), 171–205; Jacob A. Frenkel and Assaf Razin, *Fiscal Policies and Real Exchange Rates in the World Economy*, NBER Working Paper no. 2065 (Cambridge, Mass.: National Bureau of Economic Research, 1986).
15. Marc Levinson, "Economic Policy: The Old Tools Won't Work," *Dun's Business Month*, 129:1 (Jan. 1987):30–33.

16. See, for example, Ronald I. McKinnon, "Monetary and Exchange Rate Policies for International Financial Stability: A Proposal," *Journal of Economic Perspectives* 2:1 (Winter 1988):83-103.
17. Williamson, *The Exchange Rate System;* Jacob A. Frenkel and Morris Goldstein, *A Guide to Target Zones,* NBER Working Paper no. 2113 (Cambridge, Mass.: National Bureau of Economic Research, 1986).
18. Jeffrey A. Frenkel and Katharine Rockett, "International Macroeconomic Policy Coordination When Policy-Makers Do Not Agree on the True Model," *American Economic Review* 78 (1988); Stanley Fischer, "International Macroeconomics" in *International Policy Coordination,* ed. Martin Feldstein (Chicago: University of Chicago Press, 1988).
19. "European Monetary System," *The Economist,* July 4, 1987, p. 21.
20. Warwick J. McKibbin and Jeffrey D. Sachs, *Comparing the Global Performance of Alternative Exchange Arrangements,* NBER Working Paper no. 2024 (Cambridge, Mass.: National Bureau of Economic Research, 1986).

Chapter 8
The New Trade Theory

1. Gary Clyde Hufbauer and Howard Rosen, *Trade Policy for Troubled Industries* (Washington, D.C.: Institute for International Economics, 1985), chap. 5.
2. Paul R. Krugman, "Increasing Returns, Monopolistic Competition, and International Trade," *Journal of International Economics* 9:4 (Nov. 1979): 469–79.
3. Gene M. Grossman and J. David Richardson, *Strategic Trade Policy: A Survey of Issues and Early Analysis,* Special Papers in International Economics, no. 15 (Princeton: Princeton University International Finance Section, 1985), 1.
4. Jonathan Eaton and Gene M. Grossman, "Optimal Trade and Industrial Policy under Oligopoly," *Quarterly Journal of Economics* 101:2 (May 1986):383–406.
5. James A. Brander and Barbara J. Spencer, "Strategic Commitment with R & D: The Symmetric Case," *Bell Journal of Economics* 14:1 (Spring 1983): 371–89.
6. Avinash K. Dixit and Albert S. Kyle, "The Use of Protection and Subsidies for Entry Promotion and Deterrence," *American Economic Review* 75:1 (March 1985):139–52.
7. Julio J. Rotemberg and Garth Saloner, *Quotas and the Stability of Implicit Collusion,* NBER Working Paper no. 1948 (Cambridge, Mass.: National Bureau of Economic Research, 1986).

8. For an interesting if problematic attempt to undertake such a calculation, see Richard Baldwin and Paul R. Krugman, *Market Access and International Competition: A Simulation Study of 16K Random Access Memories,* NBER Working Paper no. 1936 (Cambridge, Mass.: National Bureau of Economic Research, 1986).

9. Kala Krishna, *High Tech Trade Policy,* NBER Working Paper no. 2182 (Cambridge, Mass.: National Bureau of Economic Research, 1987).

10. Paul R. Krugman, *Increasing Returns and the Theory of International Trade,* NBER Working Paper no. 1752 (Cambridge, Mass.: National Bureau of Economic Research, 1985).

11. Ira C. Magaziner and Robert B. Reich, *Minding America's Business* (New York: Harcourt Brace Jovanovich, 1982).

12. Paul R. Krugman, "Targeted Industrial Policies: Theory and Evidence," in *The New Protectionist Threat to World Welfare,* ed. Dominick Salvatore (New York: Elsevier Science Publishing, 1987), 281.

13. For an argument that some high-technology industries may meet the criteria for welfare-enhancing intervention, see Rachel McCulloch, *The Challenge to U.S. Leadership in High-Technology Industries,* NBER Working Paper no. 2513 (Cambridge, Mass.: National Bureau of Economic Research, 1988).

Chapter 9
Antitrust Reconsidered

1. *United States* v. *Von's Grocery Co.,* 384 U.S. 270 (1966).

2. *FTC* v. *Procter & Gamble Co.,* 386 U.S. 568 (1967).

3. See Eleanor M. Fox, "The ITT Antitrust Cases," *Conference Board Record* 9:6 (June 1972):34–44.

4. George J. Stigler, "A Theory of Oligopoly," *Journal of Political Economy* 72:1 (Feb. 1964), reprinted in Stigler, *The Organization of Industry* (Homewood, Ill.: Richard D. Irwin, 1968).

5. See, for example, Oliver Williamson, "Economies as an Antitrust Defense: The Welfare Tradeoffs," *American Economic Review* 58:1 (March 1968):18–36.

6. Yale Brozen, *Concentration, Mergers, and Public Policy* (New York: Macmillan, 1982), 57.

7. Richard A. Posner, *Economic Analysis of Law* (Boston: Little, Brown, 1972), chap. 7; Robert H. Bork, *The Antitrust Paradox* (New York: Basic Books, 1978), chap. 10.

8. W.J. Baumol and R.D. Willig, "Fixed Cost, Sunk Cost, Entry Barriers and Sustainability of Monopoly," *Quarterly Journal of Economics* 96 (1981):405–32; W.J. Baumol, J.C. Panzar, and R.D. Willig, *Contestable Markets and the*

Theory of Industry Structure (New York: Harcourt Brace Jovanovich, 1982).

9. Bork, *The Antitrust Paradox*, chap. 13.

10. Federal Trade Commission, "Statement Concerning Horizontal Mergers," June 14, 1982.

11. U.S. Department of Justice, "Merger Guidelines," June 14, 1984.

12. See the Department of Justice's friend of the court brief in *Monsanto Co. v. Spray-Rite Service Corporation*, U.S. Supreme Court no. 82–914.

13. U.S. Department of Justice, "Vertical Restraint Guidelines," Jan. 23, 1985.

14. *BNA Antitrust and Trade Regulation Reporter*, 50:1253, (Feb. 20, 1986), special supplement.

15. Marc Levinson, "Antitrust Isn't Dead," *Dun's Business Month* 127:5 (May 1986):36–39. Interestingly, Robert H. Bork, a leader of the law and economics movement, warned presciently of the risks of attempting quantification, cautioning that "it is precisely the introduction of an attempt to quantify economies that would make the law even more arbitrary than it need be" (*The Antitrust Paradox*, 129).

16. Dennis W. Carlton, William M. Landes, and Richard A. Posner, "Benefits and Costs of Airline Mergers: A Case Study," *Bell Journal of Economics* 11:1 (Spring 1980):65–83.

17. Elizabeth E. Bailey and Jeffrey R. Williams, "Sources of Economic Rent in the Deregulated Airline Industry" (Graduate School of Industrial Administration, Carnegie-Mellon University, 1986, mimeo); Steven A. Morrison and Clifford Winston, "Empirical Implications and Tests of the Contestability Hypothesis," *Journal of Law & Economics* 30:1 (April 1987):53–65.

18. Joseph E. Stiglitz and Partha Dasgupta, "Sunk Costs, Competition and Welfare" (Princeton University, 1985, mimeo).

19. William J. Baumol and Robert D. Willig, "Contestability: Developments Since the Book," *Oxford Economic Papers* 38:3 (supp) (Nov. 1986):10.

20. Lester Telser, "Why Should Manufacturers Want Fair Trade?" *Journal of Law and Economics*, 3:1 (Jan. 1960):86–104.

21. G.F. Mathewson and R.A. Winter, "An Economic Theory of Vertical Restraints," *Rand Journal of Economics* 15:1 (Spring 1984):27–38.

22. William S. Comanor, "Vertical Price-Fixing, Vertical Market Restrictions, and the New Antitrust Policy," *Harvard Law Review* 98 (1985):983–1002; F.M. Scherer, "The Economics of Vertical Restraints," *Antitrust Law Journal* 52 (1983):687.

23. William S. Comanor and H.E. Frech III, "The Competitive Effects of Vertical Agreements," *American Economic Review* 75:3 (June 1985):539–46. See also the comments on this line of reasoning in *American Economic Review* 77:5 (Dec. 1987):1057–72.

24. Steven C. Salop, "Strategic Entry Deterrence," *American Economic Review, Papers and Proceedings* 69:2 (May 1979):335–38; Steven C. Salop and David T. Scheffman, "Raising Rivals' Costs," *American Economic Review, Papers and Proceedings* 73:2 (May 1983):267–71.

25. Michael L. Katz, "The Welfare Effects of Third-Degree Price Discrimination in Intermediate Goods Markets," *American Economic Review* 77:1 (March 1987):154–67.

26. B. Douglas Bernheim, "Strategic Deterrence of Sequential Entry into an Industry," *Rand Journal of Economics* 15:1 (Spring 1984):1–11.

Chapter 10
That Puzzling Business Cycle

1. Arthur F. Burns, *Stepping Stones towards the Future* (New York: National Bureau of Economic Research, 1947), cited in *The American Business Cycle: Continuity and Change* ed., Robert J. Gordon, (Chicago: University of Chicago Press, 1986).

2. John Y. Campbell and N. Gregory Mankiw, "Are Output Fluctuations Transitory?" *Quarterly Journal of Economics* 102:4 (Nov. 1987):857–80.

3. Otto Eckstein and Allen Sinai, "The Mechanisms of the Business Cycle in the Postwar Era," in *The American Business Cycle*, ed. Gordon, 39–120. For a study of income distribution across the business cycle, see Rebecca M. Blank, *Disaggregating the Effect of the Business Cycle on the Distribution of Income*, NBER Working Paper no. 2397 (Cambridge, Mass.: National Bureau of Economic Research, 1987).

4. Milton Friedman and Anna J. Schwartz, *A Monetary History of the United States* (Princeton: Princeton University Press, 1963).

5. Robert E. Lucas, Jr., "An Equilibrium Model of the Business Cycle," *Journal of Political Economy* 83:4 (Dec. 1975):1113–46.

6. J. Bradford DeLong and Lawrence H. Summers, "The Changing Cyclical Variability of Economic Activity in the United States," in *The American Business Cycle*, ed. Gordon, 679–719; Eckstein and Sinai, "Mechanisms of the Business Cycle." For a controversial argument that the economy is no more stable now than it used to be, see Christina Romer, "Is the Stabilization of the Postwar Economy a Figment of the Data?" *American Economic Review* 76:3 (June 1986):314–34.

7. Edward C. Prescott, "Theory Ahead of Business Cycle Measurement," *Federal Reserve Bank of Minneapolis Quarterly Review* 10:4 (Fall 1986):9–22.

8. Robert G. King and Charles I. Plosser, "Money, Credit and Prices in a Real Business Cycle," *American Economic Review* 74:3 (June 1984):363–80.

9. The initial article on real business cycle theory was Finn E. Kydland and Edward C. Prescott, "Time to Build and Aggregate Fluctuations," *Econometrica* 50:3 (Jan. 1982):1345–70. For less technical interpretations, see Marc Lev-

inson, "Is There Really a Business Cycle," *Dun's Business Month* 128:6 (Dec. 1986):56–57, or Karen Pennar, "Growth without End? Amen, Says One Theory," *Business Week*, March 2, 1987, pp. 100–101.

10. John B. Long, Jr. and Charles I. Plosser, "Sectoral vs. Aggregate Shocks in the Business Cycle," *American Economic Review, Papers and Proceedings* 77:2 (May 1987):333–36.

11. Katharine G. Abraham and Lawrence F. Katz, "Cyclical Unemployment: Sectoral Shifts or Aggregate Disturbances?" *Journal of Political Economy* 94:3 (Aug. 1986):507–22.

12. Matthew D. Shapiro, *Supply Shocks in Macroeconomics*, NBER Working Paper no. 2146 (Cambridge, Mass.: National Bureau of Economic Research, 1987).

13. N. Gregory Mankiw, "Small Menu Costs and Large Business Cycles: A Macroeconomic Model of Monopoly," *Quarterly Journal of Economics* 100:2 (May 1985):529–37; Olivier Jean Blanchard and Nobuhiro Kiyotaki, "Monopolistic Competition and the Effects of Aggregate Demand," *American Economic Review* 77:4 (Sept. 1987):647–66.

14. Bruce Greenwald and Joseph E. Stiglitz, *Money, Imperfect Information and Economic Fluctuations*, NBER Working Paper no. 2188 (Cambridge, Mass.: National Bureau of Economic Research, 1987).

15. Ben Bernanke and Mark Gertler, *Agency Costs, Collateral, and Business Fluctuations*, NBER Working Paper no. 2015 (Cambridge, Mass.: National Bureau of Economic Research, 1986).

16. Barry Eichengreen and Richard Portes, "The Anatomy of Financial Crises," in *Threats to International Financial Stability*, ed. R. Portes and A. Swoboda (New York: Cambridge University Press, 1987).

Chapter 11
The Lessons of the New Activist Economics

1. Julio Rotemberg, "The New Keynesian Microfoundations," *NBER Macroeconomics Annual 1987*, ed. Stanley Fischer (Chicago: University of Chicago Press, 1987).

2. N. Gregory Mankiw and Lawrence H. Summers, "Money Demand and the Effects of Fiscal Policies," *Journal of Money, Credit, and Banking* 18:4 (Nov. 1986):415–29.

3. Irving Kristol, "Rationalism in Economics," in *The Crisis in Economic Theory*, ed. Daniel Bell and Irving Kristol (New York: Basic Books, 1981), 202.

Index

About the Author

M arc Levinson is editorial director of *The Journal of Com-merce*, a national daily newspaper published in New York. He was previously senior editor of *Business Month* and a staff correspondent for The Bureau of National Affairs, Inc. (BNA). His articles on business, economics, and trade policy have appeared in *Foreign Policy*, *Harvard Business Review*, *Time*, and many other publications. He and his wife, Kay Levinson, have two young children and live in New Jersey.